Effective Teaching
Today

Teaching
Social
Studies
Today

2nd Edition

Author
Kathleen Kopp, M.S.Ed.

Foreword
Alice L. Reilly, Ed.D.

SHELL EDUCATION

Contributing Authors

Sara Shoob, M.Ed.

Marc Pioch, M.A.Ed.

Publishing Credits

Corinne Burton, M.A.Ed., *President*
Conni Medina, M.A.Ed., *Managing Editor*
Emily Smith, M.A.Ed., *Content Director*
Seth Rogers, *Editor*
Evan Ferrell, *Graphic Designer*
Stephanie Bernard, *Assistant Editor*

Standards

Shell Education

A division of Teacher Created Materials
5301 Oceanus Drive
Huntington Beach, CA 92649-1030
www.tcmpub.com/shell-education
ISBN 978-1-4258-1210-2
©2017 Shell Education Publishing, Inc.

Teaching Social Studies Today

2nd Edition

Table of Contents

4

Foreword

The world is changing. It is a very different place than it was twenty or even ten years ago. It is much more globally interdependent, both in business and our personal interactions. Multi-national companies are increasing. Products are made from raw materials in one country, assembled in another, and sold to a third. Technology allows us to hear about events taking place around the world instantaneously. Nobel prizes now are given to teams of people in many different countries working together on problems looking for solutions. Participating in this global culture requires collaboration and communication.

The world continues to change. A different set of skills is required to be an active citizen and employee in today's world. Yet, our schools today are largely the same model that has been in place since the turn of the century. They represent the factory model of the industrial age. As the United States moves into the information age a realization exists that in the quest for that one right answer on a test, critical and creative thinking skills needed for problem solving are not being fostered in our students. *Teaching Social Studies Today, 2nd Edition*, provides teachers with models of how to build these higher level thinking skills needed in today's environment.

As far back as 1916, John Dewey expressed concerns about the danger of creating a gap between what is learned in school and what is needed to be a productive citizen in the world. Dewey wrote about the need to prepare students for the world in which they will live. Given the rapidly changing world that we live in today, an urgency for education reform comes from many arenas. In this age of Google, the teacher no longer holds all knowledge. Many suggested reforms encourage an instructional shift to increase student engagement and promote the development of what are commonly known as "the 5Cs," critical and creative thinking, collaboration, communication, and citizenship. In this book, Kathleen Kopp offers numerous suggestions for classroom teachers to engage their students in these skills.

The National Council for the Social Studies describes social studies as "an interdisciplinary exploration of the social sciences and humanities, including civics, economics, geography, and history in order **to develop responsible, informed and engaged citizens** and to foster civic, economic, global, and historical literacy" (2011, para. 2). In this book, Kopp provides suggested activities that support this shift in instruction. The format of the book supports many of the reforms being encouraged, such as its connections to literacy, student engagement, and multiple forms of assessment. Readers are given practical examples to engage students in their learning and provide the skills needed in today's changing world.

Students must be prepared for their futures, not our pasts. Dewey's words are as applicable today as they were in 1916 when he wrote them. Dewey tells us to "Give the pupils something to do, not something to learn; and when the doing is of such a nature as to demand thinking; learning naturally results."

—Alice L. Reilly, Ed.D.
Coordinator K–12 Social Studies,
Fairfax County Public Schools

Introduction

What Is Social Studies, and Why Is It Important?

 "I think by far the most important bill in our whole code is that for the **diffusion of knowledge** among the people. No other sure foundation can be devised for the **preservation of freedom, and happiness**."

—*Thomas Jefferson to George Wythe, 13 Aug. 1786*

This quotation from Thomas Jefferson encompasses the true value, honor, and importance of education and having an educated citizenry. Whether it is a kindergarten teacher providing the knowledge to follow rules, a fourth grade teacher providing knowledge about a home state, a middle school teacher providing knowledge of the world, or a high school teacher providing knowledge for how to be active participants of the world in which we live, all educators play a part in diffusing knowledge and creating that educated citizenry and, in turn, preserving freedom and happiness. This is no small task. Yet, the opportunity to provide this knowledge is made easier with the content area of social studies that stretches across grade levels and disciplines.

The National Council for the Social Studies (NCSS 2013) defines social studies as "the integrated study of the social sciences and humanities to promote civic competence." Social science uses the scientific method to investigate facts and is categorized into many branches, including history, civics, geography, economics, anthropology, and political science.

According to the Ohio Humanities Council (2015), the humanities are defined as follows:

> The humanities are the stories, the ideas, and the words that help us make sense of our lives and our world, and introducing us to people we have never met, places we have never visited, and ideas that may have never crossed our minds. By showing how others have lived and thought about life, the humanities help us decide what is important in our own lives and what we can do to make them better. By connecting us with other people, they point the way to answers about what is right or wrong, or what is true to our heritage and our history. The humanities help us address the challenges we face together in our families, our communities, and as a nation.

Understanding the definitions and examples of what social studies is as a content area, one clearly sees the extreme importance and relevance social studies education has for our students and society. While no one denies the importance of social studies education, it is often not made a priority by districts, administrators, and teachers due to the emphasis on mathematics and language arts. While the significance of mathematics education and language arts cannot be denied, teachers are missing opportunities to present information through the critical lens that only social studies can provide.

With this resource, K–12 educators will be able to refocus on social studies as a core content area; provide content and literacy in the same lessons; establish unified, grade level and school-wide visions for implementing social studies curriculum; and incorporate the most current social studies framework and standards, including the College, Career, and Civic Life C3 Framework for Social Studies State Standards and today's college and career readiness standards.

Purpose of This Book

The purpose of this book is to provide K–12 educators with the necessary tools to develop and implement standards-based social studies curriculum that will help raise the level of social studies education at each specific grade level and incorporate all dimensions of the C3 framework. Using the C3 framework grade ranges, K–2, 3–5, 6–8, and 9–12, this book will provide teachers at all grade levels with the necessary components to create comprehensive social studies units.

This resource provides teachers with specific strategies for assessing and building background knowledge. A specific focus on reading and writing strategies incorporated into the four C3 dimensions allows teachers to incorporate both content and literacy within their lessons. Teachers also learn to effectively use and incorporate primary sources and other essential resources relevant to social studies into their lessons. A step-by-step guide to research, different research methods, and specific research projects for each grade range allows students to take ownership of their learning. Specific hands-on strategies and simulations are provided to engage all learners. Strategies to help teachers integrate science, technology, engineering, arts, and mathematics (STEAM) into the social studies curriculum create a pathway for students to achieve twenty-first century skills. A variety of assessment strategies provide both formative and summative assessments that in turn produce the data necessary to drive instruction.

Chapter 1

Creating the Social Studies Classroom

Social Studies in Today's Classrooms

Education has evolved throughout the history of the United States and continues to evolve in the ever-changing global world. In the earliest of American classrooms, history was typically taught within a reading lesson or a geography lesson. What a great idea! Cross-curricular teaching and using content to teach reading and literacy has been around since the beginning.

In 1785, Noah Webster was one of the first educators to include historical topics in readers. These readers were some of the first ways in which elementary school students were introduced and exposed to history topics. It would take another 100 years before history would be given a status as a consistent and relevant content area.

The state of Massachusetts has always been a progressive leader in education, from Horace Mann, who promoted universal public education and teacher training, to Harvard, the oldest university in America. In fact, in the 1800s, Massachusetts required some of its larger secondary schools to study United States and general history, which eventually led to the creation of history-focused textbooks. The founding of the American Historical Association (AHA) in 1884 allowed university-trained historians to influence the content that was included in school curriculum (Townsend 2013). Yet teaching history exclusively was not the only answer. To understand the multifaceted and rapidly evolving world of the twentieth century, more was required. This need led directly to the evolution from teaching history and the social sciences to a more encompassing social studies vision. Social studies supporters argued that to properly educate

American citizens about the country and the world in which they live, students would need to first study social sciences to understand their ever-changing societies.

What followed was the development of modern social studies curricula. This marked the time when civics replaced government as a more practical course and geography was infused into all courses with a special emphasis on physical geography. Economics had long had a solid foothold in the curriculum, and sociology was added by the early 1910s.

In the early twentieth century, advocates of social studies supported a vision set by James Harvey Robinson—that to properly understand the present, one must first study the past. These advocates urged that schools adopt social studies curriculum encouraging students to examine their surrounding world politically, economically, and socially. The belief behind this was that studying contemporary social issues would help students "contribute to the improvement of society" (Townsend 2013).

To further the cause of social studies and continue its growth and evolution in the classroom, the AHA helped establish the National Council for the Social Studies in 1921. The NCSS favored the term *"the social studies* because it meant a broader and richer definition of the field, which would include greater attention to the social sciences" (Townsend 2013).

The NCSS is now the largest social-studies-devoted association, with members in all 50 states and representation in 69 countries around the world. In 2010, NCSS published *National Curriculum Standards for Social Studies: A Framework for Teaching, Learning, and Assessment.* These standards are structured around the 10 themes of social studies (Figure 1.1). Compared to the 1994 standards, these are more focused on purposes; questions for exploration; knowledge (what learners need to understand); processes (what learners will be capable of doing); and products (how learners demonstrate understanding).

Figure 1.1—Ten Themes of Social Studies

The NCSS framework consists of 10 themes that incorporate fields of study that correspond with one or more relevant disciplines. These disciplines include the study of the following:

- Culture
- Time, Continuity, and Change
- People, Places, and Environments
- Individual Development and Identity
- Individuals, Groups, and Institutions
- Power, Authority, and Governance
- Production, Distribution, and Consumption
- Science, Technology, and Society
- Global Connections
- Civic Ideals and Practices

Source: National Council for the Social Studies

C3 Framework

In 2013, NCSS published the *College, Career, and Civic Life (C3) Framework for Social Studies State Standards: Guidance for Enhancing the Rigor of K–12 Civics, Economics, Geography, and History.* The C3 Framework was developed to serve two audiences. The first audience is the state education departments. The framework is designed to help states upgrade their state social studies standards while not standardizing the content, which should be based on specific locations. It was also designed with practitioners—local school districts, schools, teachers and curriculum writers—in mind. The intent is for the document to help teachers strengthen their own social studies programs. Its objectives are to enhance the rigor of the social studies disciplines; build students' critical thinking, problem solving, and participatory skills to become engaged citizens; and align academic programs to today's college and career readiness standards for English language arts and literacy in social studies.

What Are the Guiding Principles?

According to the NCSS website, there are five shared principles that are central to the C3 Framework.

1. Social studies prepares the nation's young people for college, careers, and civic life.

2. Inquiry is at the heart of social studies.

3. Social studies involves interdisciplinary applications and welcomes integration of the arts and humanities.

4. Social studies is composed of deep and enduring understandings, concepts, and skills from the disciplines. Social studies emphasizes skills and practices as preparation for democratic decision making.

5. Social studies education should have direct and explicit connections to today's college and career readiness standards in English language arts.

What Are the Instructional Shifts?

The C3 Framework focuses on not only gaining knowledge but in applying that knowledge in ways that will help to prepare students for college, career, and civic life. It intentionally envisions social studies instruction as an inquiry arc of interlocking and mutually reinforcing elements. The Four Dimensions highlighted in Figure 1.2 center on the use of questions to spark curiosity, guide instruction, deepen investigations, acquire rigorous content, and apply knowledge and ideas in real world settings to become active and engaged citizens in the twenty-first century (NCSS 2013).

Figure 1.2—C3 Framework Organization

Dimension 1: Developing Questions and Planning Inquiries	Dimension 2: Applying Disciplinary Tools and Concepts	Dimension 3: Evaluating Sources and Using Evidence	Dimension 4: Communicating Conclusions and Taking Informed Action
Developing Questions and Planning Inquiries	Civics	Gathering and Evaluating Sources	Communicating and Critiquing Conclusions
	Economics		
	Geography	Developing Claims and Using Evidence	Taking Informed Action
	History		

Source: National Council for the Social Studies

Connections to Today's Standards

The C3 Framework changes the conversation about literacy instruction in social studies by creating a context that is meaningful and purposeful. The goal of literacy in social studies is to develop students' curiosity about people and the world around them and to promote effective citizenry in a culturally diverse world. Studying relationships among people and the environment helps students make better sense of the world in which they live. Another important goal of literacy in social studies is to introduce students to the idea of looking at the world and current issues through specific lenses: historical, economic, civic, and geographical. These are necessary and vital skills needed for college, career, and civic life. With that in mind, each of the four dimensions is strategically aligned to today's college and career readiness standards.

Why Do Teachers Need the Framework?

There are a number of motivating factors that inspired this work:

- **Marginalization of the Social Studies**—Time, resources, and support for the social studies took a significant impact from the loss of and narrowing of instructional time in response to multiple-choice, high-stakes testing. With the introduction of the more rigorous college and career readiness standards, educators were now able to reframe instruction to promote disciplinary literacy in social studies to regain a more balanced and elevated role in the K–12 curriculum.

- **Motivation of Students**—Children and adolescents are naturally curious about the complex and multifaceted world they inhabit. But when instruction is limited to reading textbooks, answering end-of-chapter questions, and taking multiple-choice tests, students' interest fades and engagement quickly disappears. The C3 Framework addresses measuring knowledge in a way that is meaningful and applicable to the real world in fundamental ways.

- **The Future of Our Democracy**—The central role of social studies is to prepare and educate students on how to be responsible citizens. However, research has found a sad reality—fewer and fewer young people, particularly students of color and students in poverty, are receiving a high-quality social studies education despite the central role of social studies in preparing students for the responsibilities of citizenship. The C3 Framework aims to provide the education and preparation for students to become active and responsible citizens that vote, serve on juries when called, follow the news and current events, and participate in voluntary groups and efforts.

What Does This Mean for Today's Classrooms?

The C3 Framework is a great starting point. Too often, lessons, expectations, and even grades differ from classroom to classroom. Student experiences vary as well. Yet a student's experience and knowledge of a subject matter should not rely on the lottery of getting the right teachers. A framework and set of standards help make this lottery less the norm. Today's social studies classrooms vary as much as the students themselves—from K–5 classrooms, where research has shown approximately two hours per week are spent on social studies topics, to middle and high school grades, where entire classes are dedicated to specific social studies topics.

Spiral Curriculum

Jerome Bruner first described the concept of spiral education, or spiral curriculum, in the 1960s. The essence of a spiral curriculum is eliminating boundaries and obstacles between grade levels when it comes to teaching content. Ultimately, every teacher has the same goal—to provide the best education and support for students. In social studies curriculum, the themes and principles are too often similar, if not identical, from grade level to grade level. The difference between grade levels is based on content and rigor. So if each educator teaching a social studies lesson is trying to teach the same concept as others, should teachers not build lessons and units to support students as they move from one grade level to the next? Imagine if a student begins learning concepts in kindergarten and those same concepts are reinforced year after year. Once that student reaches high school, he or she will be ready to tackle complex issues based on the learning provided throughout that student's K–8 education. This is the basic premise of spiral education.

The key features of a spiral curriculum are revisiting topics and increasing levels of difficulty. New learning is related to previous learning and competence of students increases. Students continuously revisit topics, themes, and subjects throughout their study of social studies. For example, the concept of democracy and good citizenship can be discussed beginning in kindergarten and continuing all the way through the 12th grade. The understanding that a kindergartner may have about citizenship and democracy will be simple but important. As the student moves from grade level to grade level, he or she should be adding complexity and nuances to his or her understanding of these topics.

Increasing the levels of difficulty is the second phase of spiraling education. As teachers build the students' learning on previous learning, new information can be related back. This allows students to draw upon their prior knowledge, and evidence shows that tapping into students' prior knowledge increases learning (Wessels 2012). Each time the topic or theme is revisited, students' competence on citizenship and democracy increases. In other words, teachers will provide more opportunities for growth and learning if they work together to build spiral curriculum in all subject matters. In particular, it is invaluable for teaching social studies because of the reoccurrence of topics and themes. The ever-increasing difficulty of those topics and themes make spiral curriculum a natural fit in social studies.

Compelling Questions and Supporting Questions

The C3 Framework is organized around inquiry as a means of engaging students in rigorous learning of the concepts, skills, and disciplinary tools they need to prepare for college, career, and civic life. The first step of the inquiry process is asking questions, and the C3 Framework identifies two types of questions: compelling questions and supporting questions.

While the standard(s) and learning target(s) specify what teachers want students to know and be able to do, the compelling questions provide the impetus for an inquiry into the topics at hand. For example, this standard (*Compare life in the past to life today*) could have the following compelling question: *How has family life changed since the time when your grandparents were children?* Supporting questions would then be, *What was life like when your grandparents were children? What was life like when your parents were children? How is your life different?* These questions engage students' interest, encouraging them to talk with family members and setting the stage for reading and research into family life over time.

Ensuring Student Engagement

After you've set your purpose and devised clear learning targets and compelling and supporting questions, the next step is to plan activities that guide students to explore and learn the content. The first consideration in this step is students' background knowledge. It's imperative to identify what students already know so you can make connections and grow their understandings. This topic is addressed extensively in chapter 2. In addition, think about how you can make connections to other parts of your curriculum. For example, if students have studied Earth science, they will have some background knowledge related to geographic concepts. Keep in mind that students may have learned a concept but may know it by a different name. The more connections you can make with a current topic, the more confident students will feel with it, leading to greater understanding of the content.

Next, design a series of lessons and activities that explore your questions. They may include the following:

- reading and writing activities (See chapters 3 and 4.)

- study of primary sources (See chapter 5.)

- research (See chapter 6.)

- hands-on activities (See chapter 7.)

- arts-related activities and explorations (See chapter 8.)

As you plan, be sure to include plenty of opportunities for students to talk, which helps them process and retain information. You can invite students to turn-and-talk with partners about a question before asking students to share with the whole class. This strategy engages every student in the lesson and allows for students to rehearse their thinking before speaking in front of the whole group. Collaborative activities, including research and hands-on projects, are also excellent ways to foster student talk. As students talk, encourage them to ask their own questions about the content, which helps them become independent, self-directed learners.

Most common instructional frameworks include student engagement portions of the lesson plans. These aspects of the lesson should include intellectual work, engagement strategies, and student talk. The main point is that students must be engaged with the work they do each day.

There are many effective strategies to increase student engagement. Consider this brief example outlining a series of activities surrounding the topic of colonial America, which illustrates how students can be at the center of learning in a social studies classroom:

- **Engagement:** Take an online quiz, such as *The Jamestown Online Adventure* from History Globe (http://www.historyglobe.com/jamestown/jamestowngame.html).

- **Student Talk:** Have students discuss the following compelling question with their seat partners: *How do activities and values of the seventeenth century differ from those of today?*

- **Intellectual Work:** Tell each student to complete a Venn diagram comparing life in colonial America to life where they live today.

Even with this simple example, students are reading, writing, thinking, and talking about important social studies content. As an introductory activity, students may begin to understand and appreciate life in colonial America, laying the groundwork for further study of that time period.

Finding Curricular Resources

The next part of the lesson plan involves identifying curricular resources that will support student learning and incorporate a variety of instructional strategies into lessons so you can reach all students. Now is the time to consider what materials you can draw upon for the lessons and activities you have planned. Note that this can be a recursive process—you may have built a lesson around a primary source in the previous step. As you review your curricular materials, you may discover a text that inspires a writing or hands-on activity, for example.

Some curriculum resources, such as textbooks or online programs, offer ready-to-go lessons. Oftentimes, however, these resources address content not required by your particular state standards, or they omit information your students are required to know. This is why setting a purpose for each lesson or series of lessons is imperative; it helps you focus on the essentials so you can use your curriculum resources to their greatest benefit. You can pass over pages or chapters that do not address your standards-based purposes. Additionally, you can identify the shortcomings of your curriculum program and begin to assemble meaningful lessons and supporting materials to address these gaps. You may find yourself deviating from the textbook somewhat, embedding information from other resources or modifying lessons to be more student focused.

In this digital age, finding and using meaningful, engaging, and relevant resources is just a click away. You can print online resources for students to read, use interactive activities or simulations to develop more complex concepts, or even chat online with experts related to particular units of study. Whatever the resource, be sure it is relevant to your purpose; that is, directly connected to the standard, learning target, and compelling question you have set.

Considering Pedagogy

In addition to curricular resources, you'll need to consider the instructional strategies you can employ to support students in their learning. These include but are by no means limited to:

- completing graphic organizers

- debating complex concepts

- taking notes

- holding collaborative discussions

- writing in response to prompts

- creating visuals

- brainstorming responses

- performing hands-on experiences

Some instructional strategies require students to work independently. Others may be used with paired students or with small groups of students. Still others work best with the whole class. In addition to a variety of grouping strategies, you'll want to incorporate instructional strategies that address a variety of learning styles and intelligences. Dr. Howard Gardner of Harvard University identified the various multiple intelligences beginning in 1983. As of 2017, there are nine multiple intelligences identified by Gardner. Figure 1.3 illustrates instructional strategies that support Gardner's intelligences. Note the overlap of activities, such as the movement and speaking strategies. The remaining chapters in this book offer additional strategies related to these ideas, helping you broaden your teaching repertoire to include strategies and activities that reach more students than if they were to simply use text resources exclusively.

Figure 1.3—Instructional Strategies to Target Multiple Intelligences

Type of Intelligence	What It Means	Related Instructional Strategies
Auditory-musical	Students learn best using rhythm and melody.	hearing music from a particular era; writing songs about information; putting content to a patterned beat (such as a rap)
Bodily-kinesthetic	Students learn best by touching or moving.	taking field trips; using artifacts; making models; using movement (such as "Stand-up, Hand-up, Pair-up" or "Inside-Outside Circle"; see page 23)
Existential	Students learn best by considering questions about life, death, and reality.	posing hypothetical questions; using simulations; having students write from other peoples' perspectives
Interpersonal	Students learn best by talking with others.	collaborative work groups; games or competitions
Intrapersonal	Students learn best by working alone.	setting goals; independent learning projects and reports
Naturalist	Students learn best by working with nature.	using artifacts; making connections to Earth science concepts (i.e., movement of populations and their impact on the environment)
Logical-mathematical	Students learn best by analyzing information.	classifying or categorizing information; using graphic organizers; thinking abstractly; forming relationships between and among concepts; using charts or other numerical data such as dates
Verbal-linguistic	Students learn best by reading, writing, listening, and speaking information.	reading text; using audio recordings; talking or chatting with experts; using video; making recordings (such as a news broadcast); conducting debates; paired, small group, or class discussion
Visual-spatial	Students learn best by seeing or drawing information	using maps, diagrams, photos, cartoons, or illustrations; taking students on virtual tours (such as battlefields); using video; using graphic organizers; creating visual representations of information (such as concept maps)

Differentiating and Scaffolding Instruction

The more you know about your students in terms of their learning needs and preferences, the more effective you can be in planning instruction. Keep in mind that one year's class (or one class period) may be very different when compared to the previous year's class (or previous class period) in terms of intellect, maturity, background knowledge and experiences, and skills. To offer all students the same quality instruction, you may need to make adjustments to the learning experiences you provide from year to year or from class to class. This is not to say that you need to prepare entirely new sets of lesson plans. Rather, differentiate instruction by gearing it toward students' needs offering them authentic tasks, challenging opportunities, and a variety of ways to learn and demonstrate the knowledge that takes them from where they are and moves them to where they need to be. Addressing multiple intelligences, as discussed in the previous section, is one way to differentiate instruction. Offering students choice is another. For example, you could provide a learning menu from which students choose activities. It could be a list, perhaps in the form of a tic-tac-toe board, of varied learning activities ranging from simple to complex tasks. You can have students choose a number of activities from the list, or you can assign specific tasks to students based on their needs.

Scaffolding is directly related to differentiation. Some students come to class knowing very little about the social studies; others have a great amount of knowledge and contribute regularly to class discussions. Scaffolding is the action you take to support students with whatever learning is taking

Quick Movement Activities

Stand-up, Hand-up, Pair-up— Students stand behind their seats and each raise one hand. They move about the room to find partners by high-fiving. Then, each student takes turns repeating important facts or information. For example, students might recite the three branches of government or the 13 original colonies.

Inside/Outside Circle—This is similar to *Stand-up, Hand-up, Pair-up.* One half of the class stands in a circle facing outward. The other half of the class stands in an outside circle facing in. The inside circle moves clockwise while the outside circle moves counterclockwise. Students are instructed to stop. Then, they repeat information to the new partners they are facing.

place, no matter where students are along the learning continuum, from having little knowledge or skill to being thoroughly proficient.

The challenge is to provide instructional support to those who need it, strengthen learning for those who are somewhat proficient, and extend learning for those who come to class already proficient with the concepts dictated by the instructional standards. While you may be familiar with scaffolding instruction in reading and mathematics, scaffolding in social studies has not received as much attention. However, this is an important topic to consider. Figure 1.4 lists some scaffolding strategies you can incorporate during social studies lessons.

Figure 1.4—Scaffolding Strategies for Social Studies

Scaffolding Strategy	Explanation
Fish Bowl	Divide the class into two groups. A small group of student "experts" sits at the center of the classroom, surrounded by the rest of the class. Instruct the small group to discuss a specific question or topic while the others in the class take notes and write questions for the small group. Only the students in the center circle may talk. At the conclusion of the discussion, invite those in the outside circle to ask clarifying questions.
Think-Pair-Share	Give students plenty of think time by incorporating think-pair-share activities. Give students a question or prompt and invite them to think about it on their own for a minute or two. Then, ask pairs to discuss, taking turns sharing ideas. This time allows everyone to participate and have practice expressing themselves. Finally, ask students to share with the class. You can ask volunteers to share their own ideas or those of their partners.
Direct Vocabulary Instruction	Choose essential words students need to know to understand a concept and provide direct instruction and repeated practice with these terms. You can vary the amount of review and practice depending on student need, pulling small groups of students who need extra scaffolding with the words.
Graphic Organizers	Graphic organizers help students organize information so they can see relationships. Select a graphic organizer that relates to the way the content is organized. For example, if a text is comparing and contrasting two people or ideas, a Venn diagram would be a helpful graphic organizer to use. To scaffold with graphic organizers, you can fill in all or part of the information for students who need that support while giving a blank graphic organizer to students able to complete it independently.

Regardless of the wide range of student needs, scaffolding strategies support learning for all levels of students. You can vary these strategies to best support the specific students in your classroom. Some classes may require quite a bit of scaffolding, others may require very little, or scaffolding may only be necessary for just a few students.

Consider this example of scaffolded questions for students to discuss as part of their study of limited and unlimited governments (Figure 1.5). You can distribute the questions to students based on their levels of readiness, or you can write the questions on the board, number them, and assign them to students by number. Have each student think about his or her question and then pair with another student who has the same question. After they discuss the question, ask partners to share their ideas with the whole class and take notes on what is shared by others. In this way, students gain the benefit of student talk on the full range of questions.

Figure 1.5—Example Scaffolded Questions

Question Level	Questions
Simple	What are the characteristics of a limited government? What are the characteristics of an unlimited government?
Moderate	Give an example of a limited government. Give an example of an unlimited government. How do these two governments compare?
Complex	Pick limited government or unlimited government and defend why one is better than the other. Include evidence to support your answer.

Using Assessments Effectively

The most important assessments should be used to improve student learning. These types of assessments are frequently referred to as *formative assessments*. This type of assessment tells you where students are along the learning continuum so that you can make adjustments to subsequent instruction, perhaps reteaching concepts that students haven't grasped, pulling a small group to scaffold a particular activity certain students are having trouble with, or adding review activities to cement students' learning before the end-of-unit test. It is wise to consider this essential component in the planning stages because it can help you monitor progress, enhance and evaluate learning, and inform instructional decisions during the course of study. At the start of a lesson, be sure to plan an assessment to determine the level of students' background knowledge and the students' strengths and weaknesses. (See chapter 2 for strategies to use this type of assessment.) Then, identify key points where you will want to check in on students' understanding and progress. These can be as simple as exit slips students fill out at the end of a session or anecdotal notes you jot while listening in on small-group discussions. Chapter 9 covers formative assessments in detail. Clearly, assessment is a key component to instruction. Effective teachers constantly assess student learning and make instructional decisions based on the responses they receive from students.

Developing a Classroom Environment for Learning

As you reflect on your own favorite teachers, you may not remember specific activities or events but instead recall the classroom culture and climate the teacher developed. This was likely due to a combination of his or her personality, attention to students, and passion for the content. Perhaps the teacher was funny, making puns whenever possible. Perhaps the teacher encouraged students to be part of the learning process by allowing them to make suggestions about the types of activities they completed. Perhaps the teacher thought differently from other teachers, extending learning beyond the four walls and front and back covers of a textbook. All these factors contribute to a positive and supportive learning environment for students. Additionally, attention to the physical environment and routines can provide an environment that supports student learning.

Depending on the ages of students and the availability of technology, physical classroom layouts vary greatly. Young learners need areas in the classroom to move. Their learning environments may have center stations, round tables, or open spaces for games and movement activities. As students mature, so do their classroom settings. The desks become more contained and the space more confined. Many classrooms still have straight rows of desks, one student behind the next, facing the front of the room. These types of settings make movement more tricky, but not impossible. If you are dedicated to utilizing some of the learning style and scaffolding strategies that require movement, you can find a way to make it work. Perhaps students can move their desks to the outer edges of the classroom, or the class can move to a common area for a class period. The point is, you should have a visual image in your mind as to how the class and classroom will look during less structured strategies and when students engage students in small-group learning activities. Planning ahead for these types of logistical issues will alleviate some of the confusion that may erupt without careful planning.

Routines are also a key part of establishing a suitable learning environment. Although daily activities might vary, students should know the expectations for their actions from the moment they walk through the door until the moment they leave. Routines include knowing when to sharpen pencils, knowing what to do with homework, having a signal for using the bathroom so as not to interrupt instruction, or having daily time-filler activities at the ready. All of these thoughtful preparations play into an organized, structured learning environment that sets boundaries and makes students feel safe because they know the expectations.

The teacher/student relationship is an important consideration to today's effective classrooms. Students who enjoy their classes show a greater willingness to engage in the learning, and they demonstrate higher achievement. Not to be confused with popularity, a positive relationship with students is an important component of a student's success in school. Students who know you care about their learning, care about them as individuals, and care enough to hold them to high levels of expectation will generally enjoy your class and do well as a result.

Online Resources

You can use online resources to find lesson plans from reliable and trustworthy resources. These plans may need to be revised to better suit your particular classroom, but they can provide a helpful starting point and offer fresh and innovative ideas. Here are three examples of such sites:

- **PBS Learning Media**—http://www.pbslearningmedia.org
- **Discovery Education**—http://www.discoveryeducation.com
- **National Museum of American History**—http://americanhistory.si.edu

Technology in Today's Social Studies Classrooms

Not too many years ago, teaching technology meant 16 mm projectors, overhead projectors, and tape recorders. Today, educators have moved far beyond that realm to classrooms with computers and LCD projectors, Internet access, video players, interactive whiteboards, smartphones, and tablets. Many teachers today use technology every day to teach content in their classrooms with any number of instant-access, engaging, and sometimes interactive technology resources. Additionally, technology can be used as a learning tool to allow students to conduct classroom investigations, research, and independent learning. Because technology has become such an integral part of teachers' and students' daily lives both in and out of the classroom, ideas related to the integration of this essential component of the twenty-first century classroom are included in each chapter.

Chapter 1 Reflection

1. Of each of the instructional components discussed in this chapter, which do you think is the most important? Why?

2. Choose one instructional standard that you will teach in the coming days or weeks. Plan two or three activities that address different intelligences. What will the student outcome be for each activity?

3. How will you support students so that each student will be successful?

4. What excites you the most about how technology can strengthen and support social studies teaching and learning?

5. What new technology are you interested in learning about? How do you see this new technology supporting social studies?

Chapter 2

Assessing and Building Background Knowledge

In social studies, students need to learn a huge amount of information. The extent to which students learn new content is based on what they already know about that content. In other words, learning new material is strongly connected to learners' background knowledge about a subject. For this reason, assessing and building background knowledge is the first consideration when planning for student engagement, and this chapter is devoted to that topic.

Children come to school with varied experiences that affect the background knowledge they bring to a lesson. For example, families who travel and visit landmarks with historical significance have children with greater understandings of history. However, students often come to school with little to no academic background knowledge about topics in the curriculum. Or students may have general understandings about a topic, but they have misconceptions or misunderstandings that must be corrected. Research indicates that since background knowledge is a predictor of success in school, schools and teachers must strategically build background knowledge (Lemov, Driggs, and Woolway 2016).

With this in mind, a critical question is what background knowledge do students need to be able to learn the content? Once you identify what students need to know, you must decide how to introduce topics and concepts in ways that provide the necessary background knowledge and experiences. This chapter focuses on assessing and building background knowledge, including strategies for building vocabulary. Research has shown that direct vocabulary instruction of words related to content leads to greater student learning gains than no direct vocabulary instruction or instruction of nonspecific words. To illustrate, teachers who go on and on about the executive, legislative, and judicial branches of government without having introduced and pretaught these concepts will have students with limited mastery of the information presented. Chapter 3 focuses specifically on teaching key vocabulary within the context of reading.

Strategies for Determining What Students Know

Very few seventh graders come to school knowing about the Spanish-American War. Other students may have heard about World War II or the Vietnam War, but their knowledge is vague. Young children may know a little about American Indians but come to school with the misunderstanding that all Indians live in teepees. Therefore, before you move forward with instruction, it is essential to first find out what students know about a particular topic. This will help you better plan instruction to meet students' instructional needs.

Administer a Pretest

A traditional method of determining the levels of students' understanding of a topic is the administration of a pretest. A pretest may take the form of an actual test in which students answer questions based on the knowledge that they have. Or, you might administer an abbreviated test using a student-response system—a digital resource on which you can enter questions in a program's software and display the questions electronically using a projector. Students use hand-held devices to submit their answer choices. You can then upload students' responses and see their results displayed in a chart or a table. Using the program software, you can determine whether all or most students answered one particular question correctly or if the whole class missed certain questions. By reviewing the student responses, you will know quickly where the class stands with regard to a particular topic or specific details within a topic.

Less structured pretests may ask students to simply respond in writing to the lesson's compelling question. Or you can ask students to rate themselves on their level of understanding of the learning target(s). Students can evaluate their own understandings of the day's learning target by using a simple four-point scale, as shown in Figure 2.1. Students can share their responses publicly or privately, perhaps by showing the number of fingers to indicate their current level of proficiency or by writing the number on the corner of a sheet of notebook paper or note-taking handout before the lesson. Then, at the conclusion of the lesson, students can reevaluate their proficiency levels and determine how much, if any, learning has taken place. The students' own evaluations also act as effective formative assessments, providing critical information as to the extent to which learning has taken place.

Figure 2.1—Self-Evaluation Rating Scale

- -

4 I have a thorough understanding of this learning target.

3 I have adequate understanding of this learning target, but I don't quite know it all.

2 I have some understanding of this learning target, but some aspects are still confusing to me.

1 I have little to no understanding of this learning target.

Pre-Teaching Concept Maps

Students can also work collaboratively to share what they know before instruction begins. You can give small groups of two or more students sheets of blank paper. One person, acting as the recorder, writes the concept in the center of the paper and circles it. Then, group members work together to record as much information as they can about the concept in the surrounding white space. Once collected, you will know quickly what students do and don't know; you'll also see any misconceptions students might have. The example on page 32 (Figure 2.2) shows how a group of fourth grade students demonstrated their understanding of the tools and technology of American Indians in Florida. Although the students understood the role of rocks and trees as useful resources, they were unaware of the use of shells and fish bones. Instead, students focused on living off the land rather than including information about fishing, boating, or other water resources. They also did not know the specific names of tools the American Indians used.

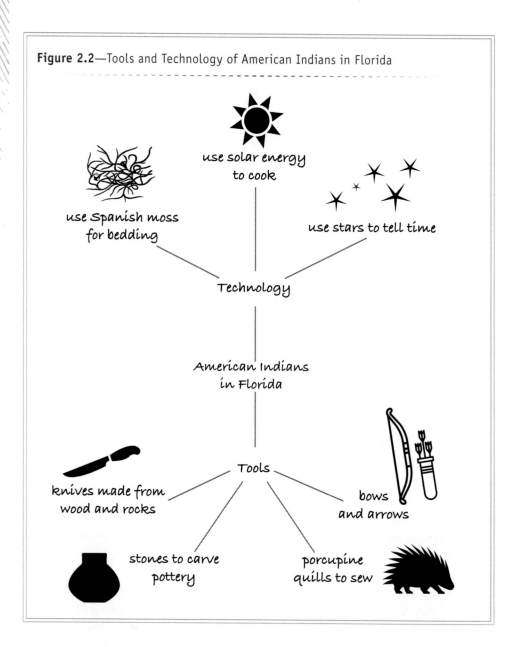

Figure 2.2—Tools and Technology of American Indians in Florida

use solar energy
to cook

use Spanish moss
for bedding

use stars to tell time

Technology

American Indians
in Florida

knives made from
wood and rocks

Tools

bows
and arrows

stones to carve
pottery

porcupine
quills to sew

Anchor Charts

Anchor charts combine the pretest and concept map ideas, inviting students to collaboratively generate ideas about a single topic. To create a set of anchor charts, write subtopics or supporting questions on sheets of chart paper. Then, post the charts around the room. Divide the class into as many groups as there are charts, and ask each group to read and write responses on each chart, recording what they know. Establish a time limit for groups to respond, perhaps two minutes. When you signal the time, the groups rotate clockwise to the next charts. Then, they begin by reading what the other groups recorded, crossing out what they believe is incorrect and adding other information they think is relevant. Groups continue to rotate through the room as you call time until they return to their original charts. One spokesperson at each chart shares what is recorded with the class. At this point, you can begin initial discussions or make notes about information to review at a later time.

KWL

The KWL chart (What I Know; What I Want to Know; and What I Learned) is an effective strategy for activating prior knowledge about a topic before new learning occurs (Figure 2.3). (A digital version of this chart is provided. See pages 205–206.) Just as readers use prior knowledge to make meaning of new texts, new learning takes place when students reflect on what they already know about a given subject. As an introductory activity, students fill out the first two columns of the chart, noting what they know about the topic and what they would like to know. (The chart can be revisited during the unit to document student learning.) The chart can be completed either individually or as a class, allowing you to discover the extent of knowledge students have as well as identify any misconceptions.

On a more basic level, you can use just the "K" column from the KWL to get students thinking about a current topic. For example, many upper-elementary students study state government. One way of introducing the structure of the government is to simply begin by asking students what they know about this topic and then record their responses. Some students may have background knowledge about the national government. Many have information about the current president or other presidents in history. They may be familiar with elections or the court system. They may also know that the government makes laws and perhaps that it provides services. As the unit progresses, the chart can be updated with new information. If students question information previously recorded on the chart, they can circle the items or write question marks beside them and then research to confirm or correct the information.

Figure 2.3—KWL Chart

Topic:		
K	**W**	**L**
What do I KNOW about the topic?	What do I WANT to know about the topic?	What have I LEARNED about the topic?

Strategies for Building Essential Vocabulary Knowledge

Social studies, as with any discipline, is filled with words, terms, and concepts that are specific to particular topics. As students gain experiences, they naturally gain access to uncommonly used content-specific words— words such as *Huguenot, judicial branch, peninsula,* and *era*. These words are considered Tier 3 words (Beck, McKeown, and Kucan 2013). This means that words like this are used infrequently in general conversation and are quite specific to the context in which they are used in social studies. However, they are extremely important for fully comprehending social studies concepts, or reading and comprehending text-based information. Students with limited background experiences are likely to lack adequate vocabulary knowledge as a result. Also, students who are non-native English speakers can be expected to struggle to fully comprehend concepts if a topic has many Tier 3 words.

The best way to teach students essential vocabulary is through direct instruction as a part of learning content through the reading of informational text. (More information is shared in Chapter 3, but a few quick ideas are also shared here.) In introductory activities, key terms come up in conversation and may be explained to students more casually. The strategies that follow are designed to assess and build background knowledge in preparation for a unit of study, but you can also use them to introduce vocabulary as it relates to specific text(s) students may read.

Red Card/Green Card

As an informal assessment strategy, you can devise statements that incorporate content-specific words. As you read them aloud, students hold up either red cards to indicate that they disagree with the statements or green cards to indicate that they agree with the statements. For example, a first grade teacher might make these statements about community when beginning a unit on the topic:

- A community is a place where people live, work, and play.

- Our city has more people in it than _____ (*name another local city*).

- A state has many cities in it.

- The state we live in is _____.

- A landmark is something that people can only see from an airplane.

- A monument is something that people build to honor a person, a group, or an event.

The activity and resulting discussion introduce key words and give you insight into students' levels of understanding. Other variations of this strategy include asking students yes/no questions and having students hold up cards with either "yes" or "no" on them to respond to the questions. Or students can simply hold their thumbs up, down, or sideways to indicate that they agree with, disagree with, or are unsure of, respectively, the statements or questions posed. To add another dimension of movement, students can stand up to agree with or stay seated to disagree with statements.

Picture Books

Many content-related trade books provide excellent means of introducing both content and key vocabulary words. For the purpose of background-building activities, these books are best read aloud to the class. They may take 10 to 15 minutes to read from cover to cover. For longer books, select specific sections or pages to read. These books use terms accurately in context, and they have pictures, charts, or other visuals to grab students' attention and start them asking questions about the topic at hand.

One way to use trade books is to conduct a picture walk. Gather a wide variety of books related to the topic at many different reading levels. Place related books (about history, culture, geography, etc.) together around the room at different student stations. Working in small groups, students rotate through the stations, scanning the books to look for pictures of interest. Students should record notes about what they see, including new or interesting vocabulary terms. Or students can draw pictures and label their illustrations with essential vocabulary. After students have rotated through the stations, lead a class discussion about what they observed. Beginning with one topic, such as geography, create a chart listing essential terms. As the class continues its discussion about the other related topics (i.e., culture, history), record additional words related to each topic on the chart. This chart may be referenced throughout the unit of study. Also, students may record these words in their learning journals and define and illustrate them as the unit progresses.

Word Webs

A word web is a visual organizer to help students build background knowledge. Look at the example on page 37, which introduces a unit on American Indians (Figure 2.4). In preparation for the discussion, third grade teacher Miss Hughes categorized the material to be covered, such as clothing, shelter, transportation, food, and other information, and she created a blank web with these categories. To begin the activity, she asked the students, "What do you know about American Indians?" As they responded, Miss Hughes wrote the words in the appropriate categories. For this activity, record all information, right or wrong, on the web. Incorrect information may be clarified and corrected as the unit progresses.

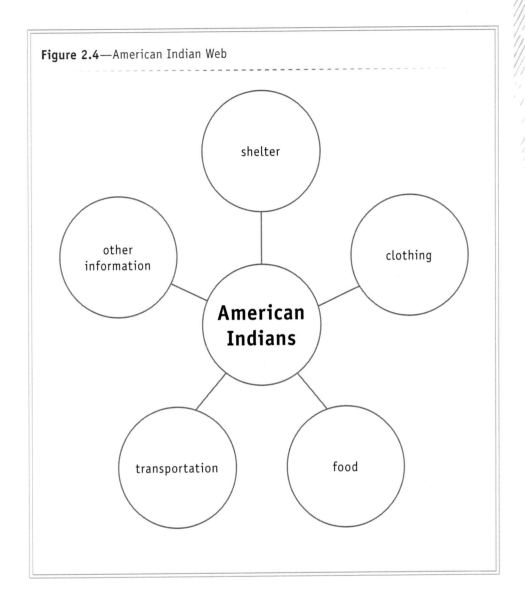

Figure 2.4—American Indian Web

- shelter
- other information
- clothing
- **American Indians**
- transportation
- food

A more challenging approach to building a word web is to have students list information and create their own categories instead of using teacher-supplied ones. If students write their words on cards or sticky notes, it's easy for them to manipulate them and determine various categories. This activity can be done individually or in small groups, and then the class as a whole can discuss and create a class word web. With either approach, the webs should remain posted throughout the unit so that students can revisit the words, adding information and correcting misconceptions.

List, Group, Label

List, Group, Label (Duplass 2011) is a strategy that introduces vocabulary terms while simultaneously revealing what students already know about a topic. Generate a list of essential words that will be used in a unit, then create sets of cards by entering the words on 3 × 4 grids that students can cut apart into cards. Give small groups sets of cards. Have them collaborate to discuss the terms and put them into categories, offering reasons for their choices. During whole-class sharing time, students ask questions of each other and defend their choices of categories.

For example, in an introductory activity on the causes and events leading to the Revolutionary War, the word list might be *taxes, Stamp Act, boycott, Great Britain, American colonies, patriots, loyalists, King George III, Patrick Henry, Thomas Jefferson, George Washington, independence, John Locke, French and Indian War, representation,* and *Declaration of Independence.* Each group of students might create different categories. For instance, one group may focus on people and events while another categorizes the words by *leaders, terms,* and *documents.* Students may also have a category titled, "Words We Do Not Know." When students share with the whole class, they explore how words can fit into different categories, which helps them see different relationships and make new connections, both reinforcing their vocabulary knowledge and building background knowledge.

Rate Your Knowledge

This vocabulary development strategy uses a graphic organizer prior to delving deeply into a topic. Students rate their familiarity with words they may or may not have heard before. This self-reflection strategy gives students a purpose for learning. It also helps them build confidence, since they will have had an opportunity to consider and discuss words before beginning a unit. To begin, select no more than 10 words from a unit of study. These words may arise during independent or whole-class reading, class discussions, or content-related activities. Choose the words carefully, considering those that are central to understanding the topic, may be unusual or may be unfamiliar to the students. Create a chart (Figure 2.5), and distribute a copy to each student. (A digital version of this chart is provided. See pages 205–206.) Then, invite the class to read the words aloud. Next, ask students to rate their familiarity with each word by placing a checkmark under the descriptor (three middle columns) that best matches their understanding. Be sure to model this process with one or two words the first time you use the strategy. As students progress through the unit, they generate content-specific definitions of the words. At the end of the unit, the class discusses the words again to ensure understanding of the essential terms.

Figure 2.5—Rate Your Knowledge Word Chart

Word	Can already use the word in a sentence	Have seen or heard the word	Don't know the word	Definition

In another version of Rate Your Knowledge, students find the words in the context of a reading selection and write the sentences from the reading that contain the words in the left-hand column, underlining the key vocabulary. Giving students a context allows them to make inferences about the meanings of the words. This also supports and strengthens their abilities to interpret words and phrases as they are used in a text, including determining technical, connotative, and figurative meanings, and analyzing how specific word choices shape meaning and tone (National Governors Association Center for Best Practices 2010).

Differentiate It!

In another variation of this strategy, you can adjust the table to include only letters that match the initial letters of the words you want students to record. By limiting choices, below-level students or English language learners may feel less overwhelmed by the extent of the activity, and they will feel more confident about participating in the class discussions.

Predicting ABCs

Predicting ABCs (Allen 2014) helps students activate and build background knowledge and make predictions about the content of the material they will be learning. It also helps set a purpose for learning. Provide students with tables organized alphabetically. (A digital version of this chart is provided. See pages 205–206.) Then, as students participate in introductory activities, they record significant words and concepts in the appropriate spaces, depending on the initial letters of the words. Be sure to model the process the first few times before asking students to do it independently. An effective way to demonstrate the activity to the whole class is to project the organizer onto the whiteboard and add two or three words, thinking aloud about how you selected them. Then, students can work with partners or on their own to record other important words from the reading or activity. Students should be able to justify the reasons for adding each word during a whole-class discussion of the text or following the initial activity.

Figure 2.6 gives an example Predicting ABCs chart. For a unit on the civil rights movement, the introductory activity was to read an article about the integration of public schools. Students were given this chart to complete as they read.

Figure 2.6—Example Predicting ABCs Chart

A–B	C–D	E–F	G–H
African Americans	discrimination		
I–J	**K–L**	**M–N**	**O–P**
integration	legislature	march	policy
Q–R	**S–T**	**U–V**	**W–Z**
	sit-ins		

Variations on this particular strategy include having students brainstorm words they think they might encounter before reading a text or delving deeply into a topic, and then adding words as the unit progresses. Students can also make mini-booklets using folded paper or note cards secured with rubber bands and by assigning each page a pair of letters. Then, they may take their booklets with them to the computer, to the library, or home to record additional words as they come across them during paired, small group, or independent learning activities.

Strategies for Building Background Knowledge through Experiences

Ideally, students would learn about social studies topics through experiences. They would take trips to museums, listen to talks on historical topics in locations where the events occurred, or travel to historic locations. Unfortunately, most topics in social studies do not lend themselves to hands-on firsthand experiences. Students cannot invite Joan of Arc to their classrooms to listen to a talk on the challenges she faced as a leader in the fifteenth century. In this particular case, and many more like it, video chatting with a famous person from history is out of the question as well. Additionally, in today's schools, budgetary and time restrictions prohibit schools from taking students to nearby museums or historical points of interest. Consequently, direct experiences with historical and geographical topics are sometimes not possible. Nevertheless, it is important to provide as many experiences as possible in the classroom for students.

Hands-on activities, such as exploring real artifacts, engaging in simulations, or taking field trips, are often reserved for the middle or end of a unit of study. Since building background knowledge is so important and these activities offer rich opportunities to develop background knowledge in engaging ways, it is worthwhile to move these types of activities up to the beginning of a unit. This switch in the lesson planning process allows students to experience the topic firsthand before they delve deeply into the content.

For example, to introduce primary students to the idea of goods and services, second grade teacher Mr. Kane took his students on a simple walk through the school (to the cafeteria, the clinic, the front office, etc.). As they walked, he asked them to look for things people do and the things they use. Back in the classroom, Mr. Kane called on students to name things someone did or things they saw. He listed each on a chart in one column or another, grouping the goods in one column and the services in a second column. Afterward, he invited students to predict why the things were placed in the different columns by asking, "What do all the things in each column have in common?" After some discussion, Mr. Kane revealed that all the goods were in one column and all of the services in a second, introducing key vocabulary for the unit.

This introductory activity gives students firsthand experiences with both goods and services and provides a tangible frame of reference to use when further discussing goods and services. Students can reflect back on their school-walk experience and the two-column chart to help them understand related concepts throughout this unit of study. Without such an activity, students will not have common experiences to reference as they learn the concepts, and the idea of goods and services will likely remain abstract and nebulous.

The idea of providing hands-on experiences for students is a topic worth investigating in great detail. For this reason, this idea has its own chapter later in this book (Chapter 7). As you read through the ideas suggested there, consider inserting hands-on strategies at the beginning of a lesson rather than at the end. Hands-on strategies are fantastic ways to engage students and build background knowledge.

Using Technology to Provide Experiences

Using online interactive activities, online simulations, virtual field trips, or videos as introductory activities are engaging ways to build background knowledge and introduce essential vocabulary. These types of digital resources pique students' curiosity and provide real-life experiences to which they may connect academic facts and information. For example, to kick off a unit of study related to the War of 1812, students might participate in an online interactive activity related to the flag that inspired the poem that became our national anthem. The Smithsonian Institution has such an activity titled "Interactive Flag" and many more interactive games and activities at the ready for a number of history topics. To find something related to an upcoming unit, simply conduct an online search by typing in the topic followed by "online interactive activity."

If your school has a one-to-one technology initiative or participates in a Bring Your Own Device (BYOD) program, all (or most) students directly benefit from the interactivity. If students don't have access to individual devices, simply project the activity for everyone to see at once. Passing a wireless mouse from student to student allows students to take turns participating in the interactivity. The added benefit of an interactive whiteboard makes these types of activities much more engaging for students.

Similarly, short videos are excellent ways to introduce a topic. Videos offer students opportunities to peek at the learning that is to come. These act much the same way as the picture books mentioned earlier in this chapter. Instead of having students interact with text resources, they make predictions and have discussions about the content presented in a video. To find short video clips to whet students' appetites for learning, conduct searches similarly to find online simulations. Type in the topic followed by "online video."

Chapter 2 Reflection

1. As an adult learner, think of subject matter that was very difficult for you to learn. What kind of background knowledge did you need to learn so you could better understand information about this subject? How can you relate your experiences to those of your students?

2. What strategies do you employ for building background knowledge for your diverse student population, especially English language learners?

3. Think of a unit that you will be teaching soon. What knowledge do students need to make sense of the material? Describe at least one strategy you plan to use to help them develop this knowledge.

Chapter 3

Reading in the Social Studies Classroom

This chapter addresses strategies for helping students make sense of text, specifically nonfiction text. Nonfiction text does not necessarily equate to textbooks, which is just one of many informational resources available for teaching social studies. To become actively engaged with the content, students need to read widely, think about the content, verbalize their thoughts, and write about what they learn. These strategies are not unique to social studies; they are strategies that good readers use with any text—fiction or nonfiction. This chapter emphasizes high-yield strategies that help students be successful with the content-area texts they will encounter during their studies.

Much of what students learn about social studies content is presented in first- and second-hand accounts of experiences. Reading and comprehending such texts is critical to the study of history and society; however, it requires a set of reading skills that is different from reading fiction. By integrating social studies texts into your language arts instruction and by teaching nonfiction reading strategies during social studies, you can give students the tools they need to make meaning of nonfiction text without sacrificing instructional time. As a result, students will gain essential and life-long learning skills that they will use well beyond their school years.

As with any effective lesson, planning begins with the standards. Since this chapter relates to reading in the social studies, reading for information (RI) standards set forth across the states today apply. Of course, the literature standards apply to any historical fiction trade books or picture books you may use, but since most of the learning that takes place in social studies is factual, the informational standards remain the focus of this chapter.

Reading for Information Standards

Here are some commonly used RI standards found in English language arts standards today:

1. Read closely to determine what the text says explicitly and to make logical inferences from it.

2. Cite specific textual evidence when writing or speaking to support conclusions drawn from the text.

3. Determine central ideas or themes of a text and analyze their development.

4. Summarize the key supporting details and ideas.

5. Analyze how and why individuals, events, and ideas develop and interact over the course of a text.

6. Interpret words and phrases as they are used in a text, including determining technical, connotative, and figurative meanings, and analyze how specific word choices shape meaning or tone.

7. Analyze the structure of texts, including how specific sentences, paragraphs, and larger portions of the text relate to each other and the whole.

8. Assess how point of view or purpose shapes the content and style of text.

9. Integrate and evaluate content presented in diverse formats and media, including visually and quantitatively as well as in words.

10. Delineate and evaluate the argument and specific claims in a text, including the validity of the reasoning as well as the relevance and sufficiency of the evidence.

11. Analyze how two or more texts address similar themes or topics in order to build knowledge or to compare the approaches the authors take.

12. Read and comprehend complex literary and informational texts independently and proficiently.

Gathering Materials

When planning a unit, consider the texts available to you. These may include:

- textbooks

- picture books (nonfiction or historical fiction)

- trade books (nonfiction or historical fiction)

- guided reading materials (nonfiction or historical fiction)

- articles (from student magazines or the Internet)

- primary sources (such as letters, diaries, or speeches)

- reader's theater scripts (nonfiction or historical fiction)

- poems, raps, and songs

- government documents

As you evaluate each text, note the information it presents, its reading level, and any challenges it may pose for your readers. Then, consider the context and purpose for which it might be used:

- **Read-aloud:** to build background knowledge, introduce vocabulary, model reading strategies, and teach genre and/or text features with high teacher modeling and support

- **Guided reading:** to build background knowledge, introduce and review vocabulary, practice reading strategies, and review genre and/or text features with moderate teacher support

- **Partner reading:** to build background knowledge and vocabulary and to practice reading strategies with peer support

- **Independent reading:** to build background knowledge and vocabulary and to apply reading strategies independently

- **Research:** to extend knowledge and explore questions independently

Here is where strong integration between social studies and language arts can naturally occur in elementary classrooms. If you have a nonfiction picture book, you can read it aloud during language arts, introducing essential vocabulary and modeling nonfiction reading skills. Perhaps you have guided reading materials you can use with struggling or English language learners to give them an extra dose of vocabulary and background knowledge. Or maybe you can use a historical fiction reader's theater script for your weekly fluency practice, giving students the opportunity to take on the roles and persona of people from the past and to repeatedly use content-related vocabulary as they reread and perform the script.

In middle and high school, a little coordination between language arts and social studies teachers can enrich student learning in both subjects. It can be as simple as having students read historical fiction or biographies related to a time period being covered in social studies, or perhaps the English teacher could do a close-reading lesson using a primary source from the social studies content.

Exploring Genres

Nonfiction has several subgenres that may be unfamiliar to students. To support their comprehension of these texts, teach students about genre, perhaps extending your discussion of literary genres (such as picture books, poems, and plays) to include informational genres (such as articles, letters, and speeches). Point out that different types of texts have different characteristics and that knowing what to expect from a particular genre can help readers better understand texts in that genre.

According to a Fountas and Pinnell blog in 2010, guided reading is "a teaching approach designed to help individual readers build an effective system for processing a variety of increasingly challenging texts over time." First, teachers determine the reading levels of students. Then, they form reading groups that allow students with similar reading levels to work together. "In selecting a text for the group, the teacher uses the level designation; thinks about the strengths, needs, and background knowledge of the group; and analyzes the individual text for opportunities to support students' successful engagement with the meaning, language, and print of the text." In this way, teachers use the text (including nonfiction social studies texts) to teach reading within a guided reading framework.

To develop students' awareness of genre, briefly assess what they already know. Do they understand the difference between fiction and nonfiction? If not, read aloud several examples of each and make an anchor chart listing the characteristics of each genre. Use the terms *fiction* and *nonfiction* when discussing reading and writing, consistently noting the genre of read-alouds as well as guided reading and independent reading materials.

As you incorporate different genres into units of study, be sure to introduce each one as a new genre, reading aloud an example and charting its characteristics. Alternatively, you can have students explore a group of books or other texts in the same genre and have them generate the characteristics they notice. As students become familiar with the different features of various genres, they develop a frame of reference that will help them read and comprehend new texts within those genres.

In the same way, it's important to teach students how to read the various text features they encounter in nonfiction. Too often, students skim over photographs and captions or charts and maps because they don't understand that these features also contain information about the topic. Demonstrate how to pause on a page and turn your attention to text features, looking closely at each component, making sense of the information conveyed, and then connecting the information to the text.

Teaching with Texts

Nonfiction picture books can be used effectively with students of all age groups—not just elementary students. They are engaging tools for introducing topics or units. Using these books is particularly effective when the students lack background knowledge. Reading a picture book gives everyone in the class a base of information. The visuals are engaging, and they immediately draw students into the text.

When introducing a picture book at the beginning of a unit, ask students if they know anything about the topic. Invite students to consider the book title and cover illustrations and to make predictions about the content. You may also preview some interior pages for text features. If you have multiple copies of the book, you can have students work in small groups to conduct a picture walk. (See page 36 for more detail.) After you read the book aloud, ask students to share impressions and generate questions that can then be used to guide instruction.

You can use other nonfiction text resources in the same way to initiate units. During a unit, provide a variety of texts to give students opportunities to read critically to understand and interpret history. To help students engage with diverse texts, offer support by incorporating strategies during each stage of reading: before, during, and after. Reading nonfiction requires a specific skill set. Donna Ogle, Ron Klemp, and Bill McBride (2007) point out that many nonfiction texts require inferential thinking in contrast to textbooks, which generally state literal facts. In addition, they often present challenges in terms of readability level, content-specific vocabulary, complex text structure and language, and text features such as maps or charts. To prevent students from tuning out and turning off when faced with these texts, it is essential to explicitly teach students how to apply nonfiction reading skills as their reading materials become more complex and more challenging to understand. The instructional strategies in the following sections, organized by stage of reading, will help students maximize their learning as they read nonfiction texts.

Picture Books with Secondary Students

There are many picture books for primary students, but these are some favorites for introducing units for middle and high school social studies:

- *Casey Over There* by Staton Rabin—World War I

- *The Butter Battle Book* by Dr. Seuss—The Cold War

- *George Did It* by Suzanne Tripp Jurmain—setting precedent for the presidency

- *The Great Migration* by Jacob Lawrence—migration of African Americans from the South to the North, beginning around World War I

- *Mercedes and the Chocolate Pilot* by Margo Raven—Berlin Airlift

- *Pie Biter* by Ruthanne McCunn—Transcontinental Railroad (written in Spanish, English, and Chinese)

- *Seaman's Journal: On the Trail with Lewis and Clark* by Patricia Reeder Eubank—U.S. expansion

Before Reading—Explicit Vocabulary Instruction

Once students have built some background knowledge and have been informally introduced to words, it's time to explicitly teach key words and concepts. Explicit vocabulary instruction increases reading comprehension, helps students communicate more effectively, improves the range and specificity of student writing, and helps students develop deeper understandings of concepts (Allen 2014). In addition, as Marzano, Pickering, and Pollock (2012) point out, "systematic vocabulary instruction is one of the most important instructional interventions that teachers can use, particularly with low-achieving students."

Because of the value of learning key words as part of the reading process, the explicit teaching of vocabulary is most helpful immediately before students read a text selection because "teaching words well entails helping students make connections between their prior knowledge and the vocabulary to be encountered in the text and providing them with multiple opportunities to clarify and extend their knowledge of words and concepts during the course of study" (Vacca and Vacca 2016). The first step is to strategically select the most essential terms necessary for understanding major concepts in a unit. Then, introduce them to students. This four-step process works for introducing the words:

1. Write the word.

2. Say the word and provide a student-friendly definition.

3. Connect the word to students' background knowledge.

4. Have students say the word and ask questions about it.

Students need multiple experiences with words to truly learn them, but this initial exposure will give them the background they need to understand the word when they see it in the context of their reading and learning. Throughout the unit, provide plenty of opportunities for students to use the words in discussion and writing. (See pages 34–41 and 63–71 for further vocabulary-building activities.)

Before Reading—Setting the Purpose

Above all else, students must know the purpose for their reading. To set a clear purpose, begin each reading assignment with a pre-reading strategy, one best suited to the students' ages and abilities. Effective prereading strategies draw on the interests of students, build their background knowledge, introduce essential vocabulary terms, and motivate students to take active roles in their own learning.

Turning Headings Into Questions

One strategy for setting a purpose to read is turning headings and subheadings into questions. Then, students read the section to answer the question. Since headings and subheadings serve as topic summaries, turning them into questions also provides study guides based on the text. For example, Ms. Johnson, a fourth grade teacher, chose a nonfiction trade book to introduce the topic of ancient Greece. She first directed students' attention to a chapter titled "Athena's City." She lead a picture walk and then asked students to generate questions about the chapter based on each subheading and using the question words *who, what, where, when, why,* and *how.* The first questions were *What is Athena's city?* and *Who is Athena?* Ms. Johnson listed the questions on a chart. After students read, they returned to the chart to answer the questions; Ms. Johnson recorded the answers. Any questions not answered by the text provide the opportunity for students to read further, consulting other sources to find those answers. Initial questions may also generate additional questions that will engage the students in learning additional content about the topic.

Previewing Textbook Text Features

Textbooks and other nonfiction materials often incorporate text supports to help students understand content. These include headings and subheadings; graphic sources such as diagrams, graphs, and charts; time lines; focus questions; introductions; keywords in bold, italics, or color; and pictures with captions. Before students can understand the content, they must understand the purpose of these supports (Allen and Landaker 2005).

For this strategy, provide students with blank templates that include empty boxes or drawings of the main features of the first page of text (Ogle, Klemp, and McBride 2007). The example in Figure 3.1 is for a page that includes a sidebar that lists a key question or a big idea for the chapter and important vocabulary, a time line and an introductory paragraph following the chapter title, a subheading that leads to more text, and a picture with a caption. (A digital version of this chart is provided. See pages 205–206.) Students can work with partners to match the text supports with the blank template and label the template with words from the text. Use this outline to discuss each text feature, helping students understand its purpose. This process helps students better understand the organization of the text and therefore the content.

Figure 3.1—Previewing the Textbook

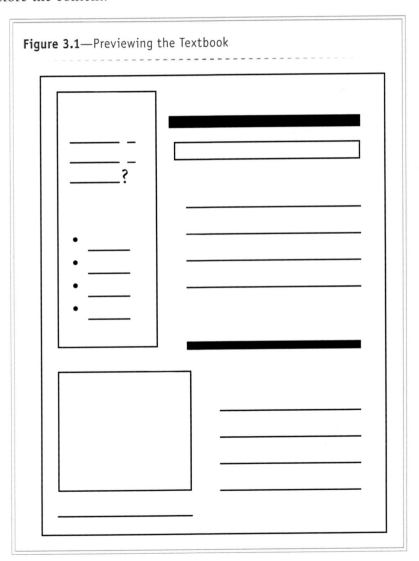

Tea Party Strategy

The Tea Party is an engaging pre-reading strategy that helps students activate background knowledge, anticipate what they will read, make predictions before they read, and make connections to information they already know. It also gets students out of their desks and talking to one another as if they are mingling at a tea party.

To set up the Tea Party, select eight to ten statements from the text and write them on index cards. Statements may be repeated to match the number of students in the class. Distribute one card to each student, and ask students to read their statements silently. Then, invite all students to move around the classroom and read the statements on their index cards to as many other classmates as possible. The only conversation taking place is the reading of the index cards. After a few minutes, place students in heterogeneous small groups and ask them to discuss what they surmise about the text from the statements, making predictions and listing questions. The goal is to have students anticipate what they will read about. Students then read the entire text to check the accuracy of their predictions and answer their questions.

Word Splash

Another engaging strategy for setting a purpose for reading text is Word Splash. W. Dorsey Hammond, a professor of education at Oakland University in Michigan, created this strategy (Lipton and Hubble 2009). It draws upon students' background knowledge, asks them to make predictions about what the text will be about, requires them to make connections among the words, and generates interest. To use this strategy, read the content material of the lesson and choose 10 key words or important concepts from the text. Then, arrange these words randomly on a page and make one copy for each student. A sample for a text about the Silk Road is shown in Figure 3.2. Working in groups, students examine the words and predict how the words are related to one another and to the topic. Before reading the text, they write statements showing the relationships among the words. They then read the text with the purpose of seeing if their predictions are accurate. Even if the predictions are inaccurate, the strategy gives students opportunities to analyze their preconceived notions and integrate them with the new information. Following the reading, students can revise their statements to include accurate information as well as to add important information. This will refine their understanding of the words and elaborate upon the relationships among the words.

Figure 3.2—Word Splash for the Silk Road

caravans

spices

Marco Polo

Silk Road

trade

Mongols

China

precious goods

travelers

politics

religion

During Reading—Reading for Meaning

Some students naturally have strong comprehension skills while others do not. A strategy to help students develop their comprehension skills is to think aloud about how to apply reading strategies to nonfiction texts. It's also important to give students multiple opportunities to develop and use comprehension skills by providing reading materials on different reading levels and in a variety of formats. The previous section discussed the need for setting a purpose for reading and engaging students with content before reading. To be successful readers of social studies content, students must identify important information (main ideas and details), make inferences, and summarize information. This section describes strategies to support students as they actively interact with texts and apply these comprehension skills.

In an ideal classroom, each student would be provided with text-based information on his or her individual reading level. The texts would take into account the students' background knowledge and experiences, reading abilities, and vocabulary development. Unfortunately, this is not possible in every situation. Some schools require the use of specific adopted materials, usually textbooks. Others rely solely on teachers to find, assemble, and use text resources through whatever means is available, such as the Internet, library books (trade books), or old textbooks. Most schools fall somewhere in the middle of these two extremes, providing textbooks that can be supplemented with guided readers, trade books, or online articles to best meet the needs of students. Regardless of the text resources available, many students need direct instruction and teacher support to truly comprehend the text set before them. The following strategies can help accomplish this goal.

Paired Reading

In many classrooms, students take turns reading aloud from their textbooks. When one student finishes a section, another begins reading. There are times when having one student read a passage aloud while others listen is appropriate. However, this practice enables students to become off task easily, allowing their minds to wander to other things when their turn is up. Paired reading is an interactive strategy in which all students are involved throughout the entire reading. In this activity, students read aloud and talk about the reading with partners. To introduce the strategy, select a short passage for students to read, note a natural stopping point halfway through, and group students into pairs. One student reads the text aloud. When the first student has reached the stopping point, the second student summarizes what has been read. The second student can also ask questions of the reader. When the pairs have read and discussed the first part of the text, they switch roles. The second student reads while the first summarizes, discusses details, and asks questions. In this way, all students in the class are actively involved in reading and reflecting on the text. When pairs have completed the reading, bring the class together for a discussion about the whole selection and have everyone share what he or she learned. As students become more proficient with the process of paired reading, longer sections of text can be assigned.

A variation of paired reading is to group students in triads. If a student struggles with reading, he or she can always assume the role of active listener and still be responsible for asking questions and summarizing. Another variation is to have pairs read different informational texts such as newspaper or other articles, primary sources, or other text resources. If different groups of students are assigned different texts, allow them to share what they have learned with the entire class. This way, everyone benefits from this new information, and everyone, regardless of ability level, has the chance to teach others something new.

Using Words in Context

When students encounter new words during reading, they often just skip them. Unfortunately, that strategy does not serve learners well, so it is imperative to teach students strategies for figuring out unknown words. One such strategy is figuring out what words mean by using context clues. As you read aloud, model using context clues to think through the meanings of new words. These are good strategies to share with students:

- Think about your background knowledge and use it to infer a word's meaning by drawing on what you already know.

- Identify any suffixes, prefixes, or root words in the unfamiliar word, and think through their meanings to help determine the word's meaning.

- Reread the sentence that contains the word for clues to the word's meaning. Signal words, such as *for example* and *including*, alert the reader to the definition of the word. At other times, the author will restate the word or use words such as *in other words* or *also called*. Words such as *consequently* or *because* signal a cause-and-effect relationship. Comparisons may be signaled by *like* or *similar to* and contrasts may be signaled by *but*, *however*, and *in contrast*.

- Demonstrate how to use text features to help understand unknown words. Graphs, titles, pictures, captions, and footnotes can all help students learn the meaning of new vocabulary in context.

- Ultimately, students will transfer these strategies to their independent reading (Allen and Landaker 2005, 45–47).

Text Coding (AKA Marking and Thinking)

Textbooks and other nonfiction texts include great amounts of information. It can be a challenge for students at all levels to distinguish between what is important and what is supporting or interesting material. Teaching about signal words, such as *important*, *main*, and *first*, helps students find clues about what is most important. However, these signal words are sometimes missing. Text coding is an interactive way of having students make connections, determine important information, look for information that is interesting, and ask questions if they do not understand. To teach this strategy, select an appropriate piece of text and display it for all students to see. Post a coding system, such as the one in Figure 3.3, for students to see and refer to. Read the passage aloud, writing the codes as appropriate: the ★ marks important information, the ! designates interesting information, the ? indicates a question, and the + symbol notes a personal connection.

Figure 3.3—Text Coding Symbols

- -

* This is important information.

! Wow! This is interesting information.

? I don't understand.

+ This reminds me of....

Once you have modeled the strategy and supported students as they attempt to code text independently, students may apply this strategy to any number of texts. They may use the coding system on sticky notes to mark sentences or phrases in the passage. When they have finished a reading, organize them into small groups to discuss what they found important, interesting, confusing, or connected to what they already knew. Ask students to discuss similarities and differences in their coding and support one another as they discuss the content. Finally, bring the class together to compare what groups found most important or most interesting. As the passage is discussed, students should defend their ideas about what is most important and what is simply interesting information. Record their ideas, list questions, and clarify any misunderstandings about the content. The discussion also serves as an informal assessment that can guide further instruction.

Making Inferences

In social studies, textbooks and other examples of expository material require students to use skills of analysis and to make inferences. Stephanie Harvey and Anne Goudvis define inferring as "merging background knowledge with clues in the text to come up with an idea that is not explicitly stated by the author. Reasonable inferences need to be tied to the text" (2007, 132). As texts become more difficult, so do making inferences. Reading skills related to inferring include making predictions, visualizing, and drawing conclusions. The trick for students is to learn to connect their inferences to text-related content and not to simply make statements about themselves or their own experiences.

Picture books are often used to teach making inferences because of their brief text and visual support. You can guide students to combine these elements with what they know to make inferences about the text. The key skill is connecting prior knowledge with new information in the text. It is helpful to model this process by thinking aloud to demonstrate how you connect what you know with what an author says to make meaning from text, so look for opportunities to do this during your read-alouds. You can use picture books but also sections of textbooks, articles, or other nonfiction texts. Thinking aloud simply means pausing the reading to explain the thinking you are doing as you read.

It says ... I say ... And so ...

It says ... I say ... And so ... is a visual scaffold to teach the skill of making inferences. As always, be sure to model the strategy and revisit it often, thereby providing students with ample opportunities for practice. To teach the strategy, provide students with blank copies of the chart shown in Figure 3.4. (A digital version of this chart is provided. See pages 205–206.) The chart should include an inferential-thinking question about the text. The key to the entire process is a good question. Read aloud a passage as students follow along. Then, ask the class to discuss the information in the text that helps answer the question. Write this information in the "It says ..." column, either paraphrasing the text or quoting it directly. Next, verbalize your own background knowledge, and write it in the "I say ..." column. Think aloud as you make the inference, and write it in the "And so ..." column.

Figure 3.4—Example It says ... I say ... And so ...

Question	It says ...	I say ...	And so ...
What can we infer about the lives of the people participating in the gold rush?	• men made money mining • women owned boardinghouses • men and women ran saloons • men used their gold to buy food, clothing, lodging	• not all miners struck it rich • women did not work in the mines	• Men and women provided different services, but both had consistent incomes.

After Reading—Summarizing the Text

After students have finished reading one or more texts, their learning isn't over. Students must realize that the information they read has value and that the value of the information is its ability to help them learn. Students should always have opportunities to reflect on what they have read and record information, thoughts, and ideas as part of the overall learning process.

Summarizing is one of the most difficult skills for students to learn (Duke and Pearson 2008). But becoming skilled at summarizing offers huge benefits. When students can summarize, they recognize the main ideas and can disregard unimportant information. They are required to think deeply about the information they read and use skills of analysis. They refine their vocabularies, and when they put the main idea into their own words, they also remember the content better. The strategies that follow provide summarizing options that students can use after they have finished reading nonfiction texts.

GIST

In this summarizing strategy, students explain the gist of a text selection by summarizing it in just a few words (Moore et al. 2010). They look for important information, eliminate unimportant information, remove redundancies, and write brief summaries in 20 words or less. To introduce this strategy, distribute copies of a short newspaper article with approximately three paragraphs. Read it aloud and then help students identify the most important information by focusing on the who, what, when, where, why, and how of the article. As they identify each component, write it on the board or a piece of chart paper. Then, model how to take these important words and condense them into a clear summary of about 20 words. You may have to think of synonyms and other words that incorporate the meaning of one or two of the words in the initial list. Once you've demonstrated the strategy, have students practice it a few times, working with partners. As students become more familiar with the GIST strategy, they can work independently. Another way to have students capture the gist of texts is by giving articles new headlines. This requires them to use the summarized information to condense it even more succinctly.

Magnet Summaries

A Magnet Summary (Buehl 2013) is another method to teach summarization. Again, students look for the most important information in a reading, eliminate unimportant information, and then write summary sentences. To introduce the strategy, use an analogy about a magnet to engage student thinking. Just as magnets attract metal objects, so do magnet summaries attract key information. This strategy works well when using textbook readings. Students read a short section of the textbook on a given topic, and then identify key words related to the topic, writing them down on their "magnet" (a sheet of paper or a notebook page will do). After reading, hold a discussion in which students share the key words they identified, and discuss why those words are important. Then, model how to turn the key words into a summary of the section, noting that you do not use all the words, since as you think about the topic, you refine your ideas about what is most important and keep the summary focused on that. The summary statement should be approximately 20 words in length. As students become more comfortable with this strategy, have them work in small groups or pairs to write magnet summaries for other parts of their textbook readings. You can have students put their magnet summaries on index cards, writing key words on one side of the cards and the sentence summary on the backs of the cards. When a number of cards are created, they become handy study guides for larger topics. See the sample magnet summary about the Serengeti Plain in Africa (Figure 3.5.)

Figure 3.5—Example Magnet Summary

- -

- home to great concentration of wildlife
- Africa
- grassland
- acacia bushes/trees
- Tanzania
- rocky
- huge
- Serengeti Plain
- major tourist attraction
- forests animal migrations

Summary Sentence

The vast Serengeti Plain in Tanzania is home to an enormous array of African wildlife and therefore attracts many tourists.

Somebody ... Wanted ... But ... So ...

Another strategy for summarizing is Somebody Wanted But So (Beer 2003). Often used with fiction, this strategy is also useful when summarizing events in history. Figure 3.6 provides students with a framework to create their summaries. (A digital version of this chart is provided. See pages 205–206.) As always, when teaching the strategy, be sure to model it before students try it on their own. After students read about a historical event, ask the class who is the main person causing the events—this person becomes the *Somebody*. Then, ask students what the person wanted—what was his or her goal? Write this information in the *Wanted* column. Next, ask students what happened to keep the person from achieving the "Want," and write the event or events in the *But* column. Finally, discuss the outcome(s) of the situation, and write the resolution or how it all worked out in the *So* column. As students practice using the organizer, they will be able to work in small groups, pairs, or individually to develop these summaries.

Figure 3.6—Somebody ... Wanted ... But ... So ...

Somebody ...	Wanted ...	But ...	So ...
King George III	colonists to pay for the French and Indian War	The colonists felt taxation without representation was unfair and refused to pay the taxes.	The king sent troops to America to try to enforce the laws, thus leading to confrontation.

After Reading—Building Vocabulary

As discussed in chapter 2, vocabulary is integrally linked with background knowledge. Additionally, key vocabulary may be introduced before reading begins, as described earlier in this chapter. After reading, students should have a variety of opportunities to interact with words to deepen their knowledge of the content. Since simply looking up words and writing their definitions does not help students learn new words, teachers must find other ways of working with vocabulary. Janet Allen (2014) advises that words be used in a meaningful context between 10 and 15 times. Robert J. Marzano, Debra J. Pickering, and Jane E. Pollock (2012) also advise that students create pictures and other graphic representations of words, be able to compare and contrast words, classify them, and use them to create metaphors and analogies. Students should have ample opportunities to use words through lively discussion and rigorous engagement. Effective vocabulary instructional practices, such as the ones that follow, can help you reach this goal.

Word Walls

Word walls can be seen in many classrooms, from the primary grades to the high school level. The focus in this book will be the use of content word walls that help develop academic vocabulary. Some word walls are arranged in alphabetical order, while others are arranged by topic. But it's important to do more than simply post words in the classroom. Word walls must be interactive. As you introduce the content of a unit, carefully choose key vocabulary words and gradually add them to the walls (Allen 2014). Keep the words posted and visible throughout a given unit, and encourage students to refer to them often and use them in their discussions and writing. Display the words on cards so students can easily manipulate them and make connections among the words. For instance, students could:

- Sort and classify words in various ways

- Identify and apply Greek or Latin roots (i.e., *agri*, *dem*, *liber*)

- Regroup words when they look for cause-and-effect relationships

- Look for ways to compare and contrast words

- Find synonyms and antonyms

- Examine positive and negative connotations

- Use them in journal entries

- Create picture dictionaries

- Identify what they each think is the "most important" word, and explain why

- Explain a word's importance to a unit of study

To facilitate some of these activities, you might give each student a set of words to cut apart and manipulate independently. Using words in warm-up exercises or at the end of lessons can provide you with a valuable informal assessment tool.

Vocabulary Word Maps

This technique helps students explore key concept words. These are words that identify a broader idea, such as *civil rights*, *independence*, or *landform*. The graphic organizer shown in Figure 3.7 was designed by Janet Allen (2014) to enable students to develop deeper meanings of important concepts. (A digital version of this chart is provided. See pages 205–206.) For example, when a group of students was studying the Antebellum Period in American history, their teacher, Ms. Lopez, knew they needed to understand the economic concept of *interdependence*. At the beginning of the unit, she projected a blank copy of the graphic organizer and wrote *interdependence* in the central box. She then led a discussion about the word, guiding students to create a student-friendly definition to place in the top box. As the students talked about what interdependence is and what it is not, Ms. Lopez filled in the ovals and boxes on each side of the word. Throughout the unit, students discussed specific examples of interdependence from their reading and learning and connected the concept to their own lives, adding to the graphic organizer as appropriate.

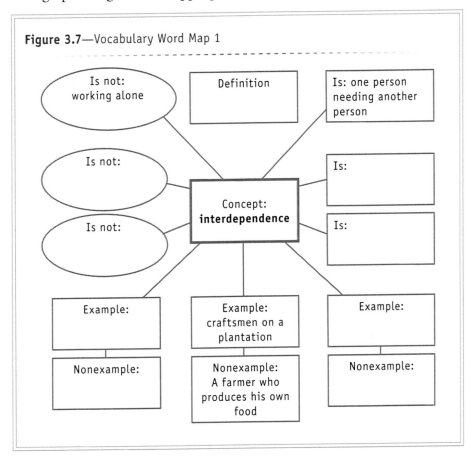

Figure 3.7—Vocabulary Word Map 1

Is not: working alone

Definition

Is: one person needing another person

Is not:

Is:

Concept: **interdependence**

Is not:

Is:

Example:

Example: craftsmen on a plantation

Example:

Nonexample:

Nonexample: A farmer who produces his own food

Nonexample:

Another type of word map, an adaption of the Vocabulary Word Map, has similar components to Figure 3.7 but may be a little easier to complete. This word map can be used effectively with English language learners and special education students because it incorporates the use of pictures. Research says that nonlinguistic representations help students think about their learning and remember information (Marzano, Pickering, and Pollock 2012). With this vocabulary word map graphic organizer (Figure 3.8), students combine both linguistic and nonlinguistic representations to learn a concept. (A digital version of this chart is provided. See pages 205–206.) They need to find synonyms and antonyms for a word, use the word in a meaningful way, and draw a picture of it. This organizer can be created by students and used for assessment.

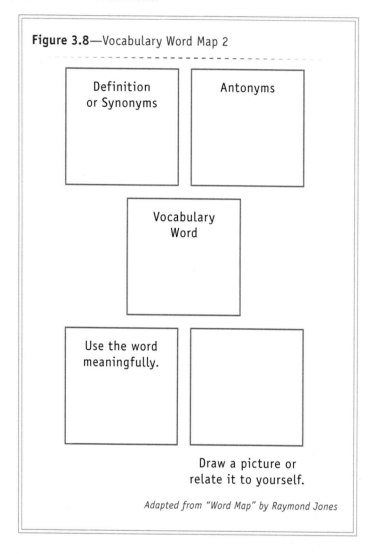

Figure 3.8—Vocabulary Word Map 2

Definition or Synonyms

Antonyms

Vocabulary Word

Use the word meaningfully.

Draw a picture or relate it to yourself.

Adapted from "Word Map" by Raymond Jones

This word map is similar in construct to a third word map, the Frayer Model (Frayer, Frederick, and Klausmeier 1969). This model provides students with a graphic organizer that helps them understand concepts. It can be used as a basis for writing even with the youngest of students. It allows students to see what a concept is and what it is not. Students also demonstrate their understanding by providing examples and nonexamples. Possible topics for a civics class might include the Articles of Confederation, the First Amendment, democracy, or communism. Figure 3.9 shows a primary example for the word *feast*. Figure 3.10 shows an example of the Frayer model for the word *dictatorship*. (Digital versions of these charts are provided. See pages 205–206.) Students define the topic in their own words, list essential characteristics, and then add examples and nonexamples in each of the four quadrants surrounding the word. They may also draw pictures in any one or more of the four boxes. In a variation of this model, students write the essential characteristics of the topic in the top left box and nonessential characteristics in the top right box. Students can also place examples and nonexamples in the bottom right box and use the bottom left box for illustrations.

Figure 3.9—Primary Frayer Model

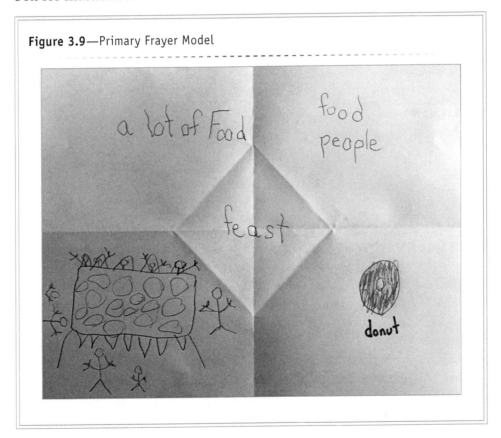

Figure 3.10—Frayer Model

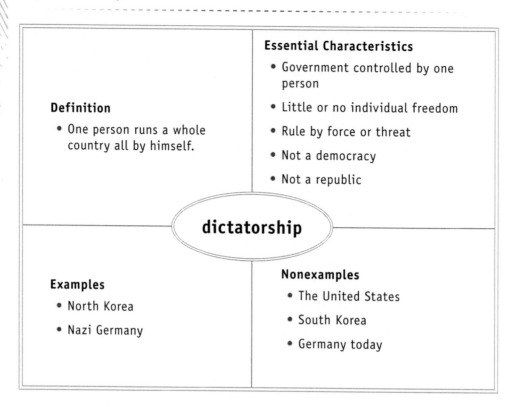

Word Questioning

Word questioning asks students to demonstrate higher levels of thinking. It employs Bloom's taxonomy to help students remember, understand, apply, analyze, and evaluate what they know about a particular concept. Consider a unit on the post-Civil War era. Figure 3.11 shows a word questioning graphic organizer for the word *reconstruction* that tenth grade teacher Ms. Alvarez created with her students. (A digital version of this chart is provided. See pages 205–206.) She placed a sentence from the textbook in the central box of the graphic organizer. (You can also create your own sentence for this purpose.) Then, students completed the remaining boxes, thinking carefully about what they already knew about the word and considering how this word helped them understand the content. They made a prediction about the meaning of the word and gave examples of what it is and what it is not. They thought about when, where, and under what circumstances they would find the word and finally evaluated its importance.

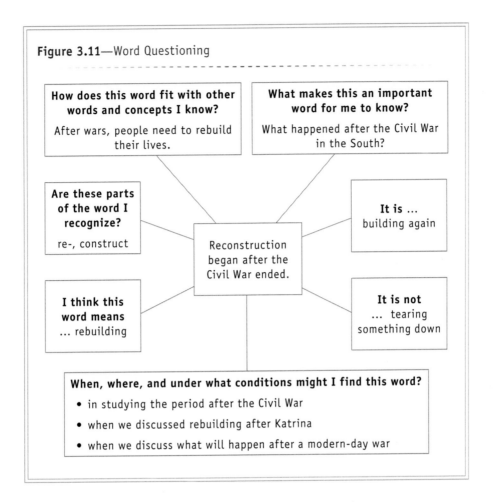

Figure 3.11—Word Questioning

How does this word fit with other words and concepts I know?

After wars, people need to rebuild their lives.

What makes this an important word for me to know?

What happened after the Civil War in the South?

Are these parts of the word I recognize?

re-, construct

It is ...
building again

Reconstruction began after the Civil War ended.

I think this word means
... rebuilding

It is not
... tearing something down

When, where, and under what conditions might I find this word?

- in studying the period after the Civil War
- when we discussed rebuilding after Katrina
- when we discuss what will happen after a modern-day war

Making Comparisons

Another effective vocabulary activity that helps students learn terms and concepts is one in which they must compare and contrast information. Research confirms that one of the most effective ways for students to retain content information is to have them make comparisons between ideas (Marzano, Pickering, and Pollock 2012). Venn diagrams are often used for this purpose, but other graphic organizers can be equally as effective and are perhaps easier to use. For example, when U.S. history students study the new republic, they must examine the emergence of political parties. The H-diagram in Figure 3.12 shows a comparison between the Federalists and the Democratic Republicans. (A digital version of this chart is provided. See pages 205–206.) As students examine critical information about the two parties, they list the differences on the two sides of the H and the similarities in the crossbar. Certainly, this graphic organizer can be used to compare important historical figures or other abstract terms. Ogle, Klemp, and McBride (2007) also suggest using a Y-chart to illustrate differences and similarities between terms. Students list differences between two concepts or terms in the top part of the Y and the similarities in the base of the Y.

Figure 3.12—H-diagram for Comparisons

Federalists	**Similarities**	**Democratic Republicans**
Led by Hamilton		Led by Jefferson
Strong central government		Weak central government
Loose interpretation of the Constitution		Strict interpretation of the Constitution
Wanted large peacetime army	Political party	Wanted small peacetime army
National bank	Had a vision for the new nation	No national bank
Pro tariffs		Against tariffs
Supported by northern businessmen and large landowners		Supported by skilled workers, small farmers, and plantation owners

Concept Circles

This vocabulary-development strategy requires students to analyze concepts and make connections among related words (Vacca and Vacca 2016). Figure 3.13 shows a circle divided into four parts, but it can be divided into six or even eight parts, depending on the concept. (A digital version of this chart is provided. See pages 205–206.) With concept circles, students must know the meanings of the words in the sections, analyze the relationship among the words, and identify the concept that ties the words together. In this example, the concept is the Great Plains. By reviewing the words in the circle, students analyze their connection to one another, and then generate the concept to which they are connected. This vocabulary-analysis strategy will help lead students to understand that inventions and new tools improved life for settlers on the Great Plains in the 1800s.

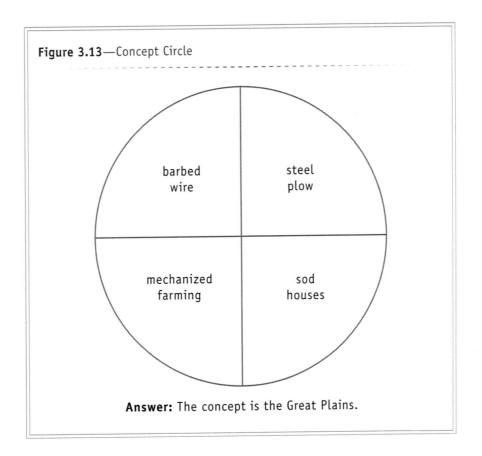

Figure 3.13—Concept Circle

barbed wire

steel plow

mechanized farming

sod houses

Answer: The concept is the Great Plains.

You can use variations of concept circles as part of your direct instruction of key vocabulary. For example, give students a circle that has words in three sections and one blank section. Students must know the meanings of the three words, understand their relationships to one another, and identify the concept they relate to. Then, they must add a fourth word in the blank section that also relates to the concept in a similar way. In a second variation, give students a blank organizer, and tell them the concept. Students then fill in the sections of the circle with words that describe the concept. They then must justify how the words are related to the concept.

Using Digital Text Resources

Any time students log onto a historical website, they will need to read information. Online resources definitely widen the range of reading material students can access to learn about people, places, events, and items of historical significance. They also allow access to information that students cannot get from traditional text resources. For example, students can take a virtual tour of their state capitals, including the capitol building, the governor's mansion, and the state Supreme Court system. This type of tour will provide students with a wealth of in-depth information about state government. Students could then summarize in writing the information they learned and create a visual representation to illustrate the most important points.

Using Technology to Support Reading

Technology suggestions to support reading-for-learning:

- Use digital audio-recording software to make recordings of texts. Students who need audio support, especially English language learners, can listen to the text before reading it more in-depth, or they can read along as they listen.

- Make e-books about historical content available on tablets or computers. Often, these books have supportive features, such as vocabulary help or read-aloud options.

- Have students use online interactive vocabulary sites to practice content-specific vocabulary. (VocabularySpellingCity.com® is one such site that supports student use of terms that teachers insert.)

- Project interactive e-books and other online texts, and use an interactive whiteboard to demonstrate effective highlighting techniques and to model annotating text.

- Conduct Internet searches for images related to your content. This supports student building of vocabulary and concept knowledge. Type in the terms plus the word "images" to your search engine.

- Have students download historical documents, such as the Declaration of Independence, the Articles of Confederation, or the Bill of Rights, to their smartphones and tablets so they can access them throughout their studies.

There is one caution about using online resources for informational learning. Typically, the text written by these authors does not take into account the language, background knowledge, or readability levels of its readers. Students who are asked to read an informational online text may need specific and extensive supportive strategies to make sense of what they are reading, depending on the length of the text, the vocabulary used, the style of writing, the amount of visual support, and the assumptions it has about its readers. Be sure to read, or at least scan, the sites for complexity, and provide graphic organizers, directive questions, or other reading scaffolds to support student learning as needed.

Digital text resources and information about social studies topics are available from reputable publishing companies as well. These resources tend to be more student friendly, and they may provide teaching guides, activities, and downloadable pictures and worksheets to support students when they visit these sites. For example, Scholastic® has numerous resources online. Their Dear America® series has links teachers can use to introduce and support student learning of history from the colonial period to the civil rights movement. The University of South Florida has a website called Lit2Go that features links to text resources about various history topics, text audio (a highly effective strategy to use with English language learners), and student activities.

While most students are skilled at finding information online, they are often unable to effectively question the material that they find (Wineburg 2016). Educators need to teach students how to evaluate everything that they come across online, from websites to social media posts. This is especially true when looking at civics issues. Thanks to the Internet, there is more information available than ever before, but it also provides a much larger platform for individuals to confirm the biases of others. In many cases, opinions or even advertisements can be published in ways that look like news. Distinguishing the real news from these misleading sites is known as *civic online reasoning*, and it is becoming a crucial skill for all people to have. Teaching civic online reasoning requires teachers to move beyond just telling students which websites are suitable and which are not. Teaching true digital literacy in this day and age requires teachers to show students how to properly question new information that they find online. The earlier students learn to question the reliability of the information they find, the better prepared they will be later on (Stanford History Education Group).

Chapter 3 Reflection

1. What specific reading strategies are most important in your classroom? Why?

2. Currently, which reading strategies do you use in your social studies classroom? How do they help students learn?

3. Describe at least one strategy for explicitly teaching reading that you will try in the coming months. What text materials will you use?

4. Who are your most challenging students? How might you use one or more of the reading strategies mentioned to differentiate instruction as you support student learning?

5. Describe a focused, direct vocabulary lesson to help your students learn new words.

Chapter 4

Writing in the Social Studies Classroom

Today's social studies classroom is full of engaging, meaningful writing assignments for a variety of purposes. No longer do students sit in straight rows reading long sections of textbooks and answering comprehension questions at the ends of the chapters. Today, students use writing as a means to learn by recording thoughts and ideas, organizing information, and reflecting on concepts. Today's writing standards require students to write informational essays and arguments grounded in solid evidence; the social studies curriculum is replete with relevant and meaningful topics for students to explore in this way. Students can also use research skills to complete projects centered on focus questions. Given the depth of today's writing standards, teachers have an obligation to help students learn and grow as writers in the content areas, giving them reasons to apply all parts of the writing process as they simultaneously demonstrate their understanding of topics and concepts through meaningful and varied compositions.

Sample writing standards are shown here. Notice the direct connection between these writing expectations and the tasks typically assigned as part of social studies units. The remaining ideas in this chapter will help you integrate writing into social studies.

Writing Standards

1. Write arguments to support claims in an analysis of substantive topics or texts, using valid reasoning and relevant and sufficient evidence.

2. Write informative/explanatory texts to examine and convey complex ideas and information clearly and accurately through the effective selection, organization, and analysis of content.

3. Write narratives to develop real or imagined experiences or events using effective technique, well-chosen details, and well-structured event sequences.

4. Produce clear and coherent writing in which the development, organization, and style are appropriate to task, purpose, and audience.

5. Develop and strengthen writing as needed by planning, revising, editing, rewriting, or trying a new approach.

6. Use technology, including the Internet, to produce and publish writing and to interact and collaborate with others.

7. Conduct short as well as more sustained research projects based on focused questions, demonstrating understanding of the subject under investigation.

8. Gather relevant information from multiple print and digital sources, assess the credibility and accuracy of each source, and integrate the information while avoiding plagiarism.

9. Draw evidence from literary or informational texts to support analysis, reflection, and research.

10. Write routinely over extended time frames and shorter time frames for a range of tasks, purposes, and audiences.

Writing to Learn: Strategies to Remember and Learn Content

Social studies content can be very abstract to students because much of the information and facts are about historical events, faraway places, people students will never meet, and new words they have never encountered. All they have to go on are the stories, summaries, and conclusions of historians and experts that have found their way to history books. Students will read information from various sources. However, without the element of recording information in a meaningful and logical manner, all these details are easily lost, not committed to memory, not used to develop opinions grounded in fact. Students can use the process of writing to personally document important points, details, and descriptions. They may use these notes to reflect, respond, and express ideas more confidently and effectively.

Taking Notes

As with any skill, taking notes must be taught directly and practiced regularly for students to become proficient at it. Note taking may begin in kindergarten with the recording and posting of information on anchor charts, drawing paper, and personal learning journals. By third grade, students should be able to begin taking notes more independently but with direct guidance and support through the use of focus questions and premade outlines. Middle school students are expected to take notes; however, depending on their experiences in elementary school, students may still need to have this skill modeled and practiced. By high school, students are generally on their own, and they are expected to have enough of a foundation with note taking to successfully apply this skill independently.

The main problem with note taking is that students either write too much or too little. Young learners struggle to identify the most important points and supportive details. They overlook text features such as bold text, headings, and visuals, which can give them clues to the main ideas of a section of text. If shown a video and asked to take notes, students will attempt to write everything they see and hear, or they will write nothing. To address this problem, provide direct instruction, taking time to stop, discuss, analyze, and identify what students should know and understand from the lesson. This process should be modeled multiple times and for various media to help students build the needed comprehension skills of identifying main idea and details and making inferences.

Note taking can take many shapes and forms. One common manner of recording information is using graphic organizers. For this particular example related to the causes of the Civil War, students would complete an advanced organizer modeled after a T-chart: one half would list the South's perspectives and the other half the North's (Figure 4.1). Students would complete one T-chart per category: social, economic, and cultural. Matrices, such as the one shown in Figure 4.2, are also popular organizers when students need to compare many characteristics among two or more categories. The characteristics, in this case, are the social, economic, and cultural differences. The categories are North and South. Once they have these ideas recorded in an organized manner, students begin to better make sense of the information and more deeply compare the two perspectives. This type of organizer makes the information more accessible to students, and they can use their notes as a reference throughout their studies. (Digital versions of these charts are provided. See pages 205–206.)

Figure 4.1—Advanced Organizer: T-Chart

Social Differences	
North	South

Figure 4.2—Advanced Organizer: Matrix

	North	South
social		
economic		
cultural		

Although graphic organizers are easy to find and use for various text structures (e.g., cause and effect, main idea and details, sequencing, and compare/contrast), not all notes need be written in a formal manner. Students can record notes using flipbooks, flap books, or folded paper. By folding and cutting flaps, for example, students can record facts and information about each branch of government (three flaps) or the three regional colonies (New England, Middle, and Southern—also three flaps). Students would write the topics on the tops of the flaps, then include specific details about each topic under each flap.

Graphic organizers and folded paper notes provide students with friendly manners in which to record the most important facts and information. However, since these documents are not bound in any way, they can become lost or misplaced easily. To keep this from happening, have students maintain three-ring binders and/or pocket folders in which to hold all their loose notes. Students completing notes electronically may keep them in files through cloud storage, on their computers, or on USB flash drives.

Another option to help students keep and maintain possession of their notes is to have them write entries in bound notebooks or journals. These types of recording systems may be referred to as learning logs or learning journals, reflection journals, or essential question journals. Students can use them to take notes, write vocabulary words and definitions, respond to focus questions, or simply reflect on the day's learning. Students can also fold and paste in loose papers, such as completed graphic organizers, directly into the notebooks so that they stay with any other notes they may have taken.

Notes help students organize large amounts of information into manageable chunks. Taking notes is a way for students to record their learning and thinking. Well-maintained notebooks provide students with means of reviewing the most important points they have learned, and they act as resourceful study guides as students near the end of a particular unit. Since they are the students' means of documenting their learning, they are not intended for grading. Other writing tasks, such as the ones that follow, allow formative and summative assessment of student learning through the use of valuable writing strategies.

Summarizing Text

Summaries are usually concise retellings of information students have read about or listened to. They require students to identify the most important information in a text and restate it in a meaningful manner in their own words. Stephanie Harvey and Anne Goudvis compare summarizing to the construction of a jigsaw puzzle: "In the same way that we manipulate hundreds of puzzle pieces to form a new picture, students must arrange multiple fragments of information until they see a new pattern emerge" (2007, 179).

Summaries generally take the form of standard paragraphs. Students restate the main idea regarding the topic and include one or two details or examples to support the main idea. Suggestions for summarizing textual content were included in the previous chapter (page 60). In addition, you might try the following variations, which all require students to identify key details about content and present them in interesting—and memorable—ways.

- Drawing a simple cartoon between two or three historical figures, each with speech bubbles stating the main idea and the supporting details

- Completing a 3–2–1 summary with guided prompts (example: describe three differences between valleys and plateaus; list two valleys and two plateaus; state one reason knowledge of valleys and plateaus is important to citizens in a global society)

- Writing six relevant details about a topic, each on the face of a cube outline

- Completing a sentence starter (example: "If I had been at the Boston Tea Party, I would have seen ... heard ... smelled ... felt .... ")

Writing to Learn: Tasks for Developing Content Understanding

Once students have taken notes and/or written summaries to help them recall content, offering them opportunities to use their knowledge in writing tasks is an excellent way to deepen their understanding of topics and hone their analytical thinking skills. Writing about content helps students process their learning, so it's wise to make writing a regular part of students' daily work. Try these simple tasks that students can do in a learning journal in less than five minutes:

- Free write about a key word at the beginning of class to activate prior knowledge.

- Summarize a partner or small-group discussion in preparation for sharing with the whole class.

- Respond to a prompt or an essential question to extend thinking about a topic.

- Pose questions that can prompt further learning.

- Reflect on the day's lesson to consolidate learning.

More involved writing tasks are also important, and this is another area where integrating social studies and language arts can save instructional time while building content knowledge. Allow students to work on their social studies writing tasks during literacy time. In middle and high school, team with English teachers to see what kind of integration is possible; even one project in a marking period or semester can be beneficial.

All writing benefits from going through the writing process, so be sure to allow time for prewriting, drafting, revising, and editing. Not all pieces have to go all the way to publishing, although it can be an effective way to culminate a unit and showcase learning. When introducing a new type of task, be sure to provide a model, either thinking aloud as you create your own in front of the class or providing a sample you've made or collected from a student in a previous year. If you plan to assess the writing for a formal grade, give students a rubric or a checklist listing the required elements and grading criteria. See the sample rubrics on pages 179–181. (Digital versions of these charts are provided. See pages 205–206).

Since the focus is on social studies learning, make those criteria primary. It's all right to consider grammar and style issues, but they should be a small part of the grade or perhaps a separate language arts grade altogether.

Keeping the standards in mind, there are three main types of writing tasks:

1. **Opinions/Arguments:** Students develop claims about a topic and support them by using evidence from text(s).

2. **Informative/Explanatory:** Students describe an event, an idea, or a person conveying key information organized in sensible ways.

3. **Narrative:** Students create stories to explain an event, an idea, or a person.

Suggestions for each type of task are provided in the sections that follow. Note that the research report is covered fully in chapter 6; the writing activities in this chapter are intended for students to do in response to their reading as a way of deepening their comprehension.

The Writing Process

Allow time for students to work through the writing process with any extended writing tasks assigned. Remember, the steps are recursive rather than linear, so it's possible students at the revising stage will do a little more prewriting to generate new content for a particular section.

- **Prewriting:** Offer graphic organizers, free-writing prompts, and time to talk to help students generate ideas.

- **Drafting:** Allow students time in class to draft their work. Confer with students who have trouble getting started.

- **Revising:** Encourage students to share their work with peers to get feedback. Remind them to employ revision techniques they've learned in language arts.

- **Editing:** Use checklists or guidelines from writing lessons to help students edit their work.

- **Publishing:** Have students submit clean copies for assessment purposes.

Opinions and Arguments

Writing an argument begins with developing an opinion and offering reasons for it. In the early grades, students can share their opinions about the best way to get to school, whether they would prefer to live in colonial times or modern times, or what job in the community they would most like to have. Elementary and middle school students can write letters to school or local government officials or the local newspaper to express their opinion on community issues. As students become adept at stating opinions and supporting them with reasons, usually by middle school, introduce the idea of an argument as a way of presenting a line of thought about a topic or an issue, and supporting it with evidence drawn from text.

Possible formats for writing opinions and arguments include:

- **Paragraphs and essays**: A topic sentence states the opinion or argument, and the body of each paragraph provides supporting details drawn from personal experience and text evidence.

- **Letters**: Students write letters to the editor or letters from one historical figure to another. Students consider their audience to determine the best way to present their supporting evidence in ways that will persuade readers to share their view.

- **Speeches**: Students craft speeches to present their opinions or arguments and then deliver them to the class or small groups.

- **Blog posts**: The online format encourages students to read multiple examples written by peers and comment on them.

Since this type of writing requires students to make statements and provide evidence, graphic organizers that support this type of organization can be helpful to students as they generate ideas and plan their pieces. A sample graphic organizer that can be used for assignments such as these has been provided in the Digital Resources (pages 205–206).

Informative and Explanatory Writing

When students write to explain something they've learned, they often ask questions and reread texts to clarify ideas because they need full understanding about the subject before they can teach it to someone else. Some ways to incorporate this type of writing into social studies units include:

- **News articles**: Students can write about an event, taking on the role of a journalist reporting on it during the time period it occurred.

- **Podcasts**: Students prepare a script explaining an event or idea and then record it.

- **Informational books**: Students can write their own informational texts about a topic or time period for peers or younger students.

- **How-to pieces**: Students explain how a daily task was done in a specific historical period.

- **Time lines**: Students can create an annotated time line to explain a sequence of events.

- **Interviews**: Students can work in pairs to write an interview of a historical figure and then perform the interview either for the class or on video.

Depending on the topic and format, students may organize information chronologically, provide descriptions, compare and contrast people or events, explain a cause-and-effect relationship, discuss a problem and various solutions, or incorporate narrative. Help students choose graphic organizers that best support the way they plan to present their information.

Narratives

Narratives in social studies can be nonfiction, such as a biography, or historical fiction, such as imagining the life of a person in a specific time period. Here are some ideas for incorporating narrative writing into social studies:

- **Journal entries**: Students can write journal entries from the perspective of someone living during a particular historical period.

- **Post cards**: Students can write brief notes about an event from the persona of a historical figure who participated in the event.

- **Plays**: Small groups can write scripts depicting daily life or a key historical event.

- **Eulogies**: Students present the highlights of a person's life and explain why he or she will be remembered. These can be presented or recorded, if desired.

- **Historical fiction**: Students can write short stories set in a particular time period, being sure to accurately depict living conditions and contemporary people and events.

At the most basic, narratives should have beginnings, middles, and ends, and simple three-column organizers can help students ensure that they have those elements in place. For more detailed pieces, such as plays and historical fiction, students may want to plan out the characters, the setting, the problem, and the plot events. Planning sheets have been included in the Digital Resources (page 205). These activity sheets can be used to help plan out different aspects of narrative writing into a social studies assignment.

Using Technology to Enhance Writing

Students can use technology resources to publish and share writing. If you have easy access to computers, have students write using a word-processing program, which makes revising much less painful. Posting information to a classroom blog or website is highly motivating for students and provides an authentic audience for their work. In addition, there are numerous online resources students can use to produce original and creative writing tasks. For example, students can use an online avatar-making program, such as Voki, to record and share facts, details, or information from historical figures' perspectives.

Chapter 4 Reflection

1. Which writing standard do your students most often use in your classroom? How can you improve students' application of this skill to be more effective toward student learning?

2. Which additional writing standard(s) would you like to have students use more of? How might you accomplish this? Devise a simple plan for an upcoming unit.

3. How do students use notes in your classroom? What challenges have you faced with regard to note taking or the use of notes to demonstrate learning? What might you do differently to help students overcome these obstacles?

4. What do you think is the best part about report writing? What strategies or ideas from this chapter will you use when you assign students their next report or writing project?

Chapter 5

Using Primary (and Other Essential) Resources

Many years ago, volunteer docents from the National Archives and Records Administration made a classroom outreach visit with facsimiles of primary sources relating to a revolutionary soldier, Simon Fobes. At first, the students were fearful of the resources, which looked daunting to read. However, as teachers helped them analyze the materials and asked probing questions, students became intrigued and came up with their own questions. Suddenly, Fobes became real for them, and they had better understanding of the life of a revolutionary soldier from this source than from any account they could read in their textbooks.

This chapter discusses how to use primary sources to make social studies topics come alive for students. Using primary sources "can grab students' attention, making them want to know about the past and helping them make connections to the present." (Conklin 2015). They can engage students in learning how people during a given time period acted, thought, and felt. Students see events from different perspectives, develop historical empathy, see the similarities and differences among people, and make connections to their own lives. Using primary sources helps students develop skills of observation and inquiry. Students ask questions, develop research skills, analyze information, and draw conclusions. They utilize critical-thinking skills and learn to think like historians, geographers, economists, and political scientists.

Exactly what are primary sources? The Library of Congress (n.d.) defines primary sources as "original documents and objects, which were created at the time under study." They are items or records that have survived from the past, such as clothing, letters, photographs, and manuscripts. Primary sources are part of a direct personal experience of a time or an event.

In contrast, secondary sources are created by documenting or analyzing someone else's experience to provide perspective or description of a past event. Secondary sources may have been written shortly after or long after an event took place. Many newspaper articles and paintings are secondary sources. Students need to realize that not all primary and secondary sources are accurate or reliable. Anyone who has created them has a definite point of view or bias. Knowing this creates another layer of analysis for students as they investigate these sources.

Additionally, the reading for information standards require the use of primary and secondary sources as students read and learn with more complex texts. When students use primary sources as part of their study of history, civics, economics, and geography, they apply advanced reading skills, which relate to text structure, or how the text is organized. Two common text structures used in social studies content are chronological and cause/effect. As students read a variety of materials, they learn to identify and compare text structures. Point of view is another common reading-for-information standard. To demonstrate mastery of this objective, students must first identify the author/creator's point of view. Then, they can analyze how the author uses words to shape the content and style of the text. In fourth grade, a point-of-view standard might explicitly mention the use of firsthand and secondhand accounts of events. If students are reading firsthand accounts of events, they are using primary sources. Charts, maps, time lines, and so forth also come into play with the reading for information standards, in which students are to use graphical representations to help them analyze and comprehend text. The more varieties of reading materials students are exposed to, including primary source documents, the more they can analyze instructional content and apply critical-reading skills.

This chapter contains strategies for examining photographs, paintings, written documents, maps, posters, and cartoons. Chapters that follow include the use of artifacts, music, and film as primary sources students may use during their studies.

Locating Primary Sources

The first step is locating primary sources. Some publishing companies produce instructional materials that include a variety of primary sources in response to the demand for these as valuable instructional tools. Social studies textbook programs often present primary sources through posters, digital files, or web links. Most textbooks include visuals, so students likely may find historic portrayals or historical documents within the pages of their textbooks. Additionally, many trade books can have combinations of drawings and photographs or other primary sources embedded within the text. These are all accessible resources found in your school or local libraries. But don't forget the vast and seemingly endless quantity and variety of resources available on the Internet. Reliable sites such as the Library of Congress, the National Archives, and the National Museum of American History are great first stops when looking for that one perfect something to use to enhance a unit. The list below (Figure 5.1) may help you get started searching for valuable primary sources to use with your students.

Figure 5.1—Online Repositories of Primary Sources

Colonial Williamsburg	http://www.history.org
Library of Congress	http://www.loc.gov
Library of Congress American Memory	http://memory.loc.gov/ammem/index.html
Library of Congress Teaching with Primary Sources Program	http://www.loc.gov/teachers/tps/
National Archives	http://www.archives.gov
National Archives Document Analysis Worksheets	http://www.archives.gov/education/lessons/worksheets
National World War II Museum: New Orleans	http://www.nationalww2museum.org
Our Documents: 100 Milestone Documents	http://www.ourdocuments.gov
Smithsonian Education	http://www.smithsonianeducation.org/
Smithsonian Source Resources for Teaching American History	http://www.smithsoniansource.org

Using Visuals to Teach Content

Students of all ages enjoy looking at photographs, which are perfect for introducing very young children to the concept of primary sources. When they bring photos of themselves as babies and preschoolers, they are beginning to understand that these are their own primary sources. They can also bring pictures of their parents, grandparents, and great-grandparents when they were young children, and compare and contrast the photographs. These pictures lead to interesting discussions regarding how people change over time. In other photographs, young children can examine changes in clothing, housing, transportation, schooling, work, and leisure activities. Young children delight in comparing their lives with lives of people long ago and can easily complete two-column data retrieval charts. Figure 5.2 graphically depicts a way to compare a student's own life to the life of a fictional character from a different time period. (A digital version of this chart is provided. See pages 205–206.)

Figure 5.2—Comparing Now and Long Ago

	Now	Long Ago
food		
clothing		
housing		
activities		

As young learners examine other types of photographs, the following graphic organizer, Figure 5.3, is a simple way to focus their thinking. (A digital version of this chart is provided. See pages 205–206.)

Figure 5.3—Picture Study

Describe the People	Describe the Objects	Describe the Actions

What do you think about this picture?

- I think ...

- I wonder ...

- A good title for this picture is ...

More sophisticated questions for older students include the following:

- What things in the photograph are familiar to you?

- When was this photograph taken? (time period, season)

- Why was this photograph taken?

- What is the point of view of the photographer?

- How does the photograph make you feel?

- Why is this photograph historically significant?

- What can you infer from this photograph?

- If this person could speak, what do you think he or she would say?

- What questions do you have?

- How could you find the answers to your questions?

Historical events are sometimes portrayed in paintings instead of photographs. Paintings are often rich in detail and information, and they offer opportunities for students to examine history from the artists' perspectives. For example, students might examine the painting of George Washington's family by Edward Savage (Figure 5.4). This painting depicts Washington, his wife, and two Custis grandchildren seated at a table looking at a map, a plan for the Federal City. Washington's slave, William Lee, stands in the background. Students can make observations and discuss questions similar to the ones asked of photos, or they may respond to more specific questions such as the ones included with the figure.

Figure 5.4—*The Washington Family* by Edward Savage

Source: National Gallery of Art

Sample questions to ask with this painting may include:

- Who do you think all the people in the painting are?
- What kind of clothes are they wearing? Why is George Washington wearing a uniform?
- How do you know if the family is rich or poor?
- Why do you think there's a map and a globe in the picture?
- Who do you think the man in the back of the picture is?
- How is this picture similar or different from a picture of your family?
- What questions do you have about this painting?
- Where might you find answers to your questions?

Students can also use paintings of the same subject but from different points in history to analyze, compare and contrast, make inferences, and draw conclusions about events and people from history. For example, students might observe this painting of George Washington (Lansdowne portrait) by Gilbert Stuart (Figure 5.5). The objects included in the portrait are symbolic of what Washington viewed as his important legacy.

Figure 5.5—*George Washington* by Gilbert Stuart

Source: Library of Congress Prints and Photographs Division

Students can compare this to a painting of Washington as the commander in the Revolutionary War (Figure 5.6). One product outcome might be to have students write dialogues as if they were George Washington during each point in his life. Their dialogue would be expected to include insight into how his view may have changed as he grew older.

Figure 5.6—George Washington Portrait by Charles W. Peale

Source: Library of Congress Prints and Photographs Division

Using Written Documents to Teach Content

Often, primary teachers are hesitant to use text-based primary sources because they believe that their students cannot read text with such a high level of complexity, as is the case with most historical documents. However, many primary sources are appealing and accessible to young children. You know your students best and can determine whether a text is too complex for them to comprehend, even with instructional support. Remember that students deserve and value opportunities to analyze authentic written documents. And some documents, although the text may be complex, come in a variety of formats that students will willingly tackle. These include, but are certainly not limited to, diaries, wills, paper money, census records, newspaper articles, and letters.

When using a written document, choose it carefully to ensure that it meets your learning objectives. Take into account the document's length, style, readability level, vocabulary usage, and the abilities and background knowledge of your students. Students will enjoy seeing a copy of an original document, and they should have the opportunity to spend time deciphering it. However, depending on the document and abilities of the students, typed copies of the text may provide the text support students need to learn from it. If the document is lengthy, you can use just the essential excerpt(s) embedded within the document. Also, before having students tackle a document, build any necessary background knowledge and pre-teach essential vocabulary words. (See chapter 2 for ideas.)

The following is a list of some generic questions to use with most documents:

- What type of written document is this?

- Who wrote it, and when was it written?

- Who is the audience for the document?

- What is the purpose of the document?

- What three things did the author write that you think are important?

- What can you learn about life at the time the document was written?

- What unanswered questions do you still have?

Questions are adapted from the National Archives and Records Administration's Document Analysis Worksheets.

To illustrate the value of using written documents, consider the following letter (Figure 5.7) to President Dwight Eisenhower, which was written by a child. Michael Rosenberg had previously written the president asking that Eisenhower let his parents out of prison. His parents were the infamous Julius and Ethel Rosenberg. At the point in history when this letter was written, the Rosenbergs were heading toward execution. Using this document brings a personal touch to what might otherwise be considered just another event in a long line of historical events through time. Such documents help students understand that history has many stories to tell outside of those told by textbook authors and that every event can be viewed from several different perspectives. The use of this type of document, very simple in nature, opens a whole world of analytical thinking and learning on the part of students.

Figure 5.7—Telegram to President Eisenhower

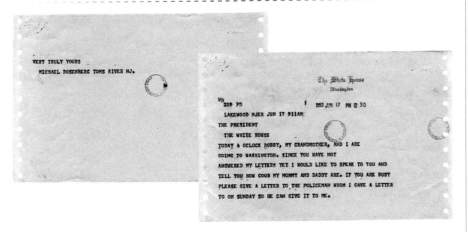

1953 June 17 p.m. 12:50
The President
The White House

   Today 4 o'clock Robby, my grandmother, and I are going to Washington. Since you have not answered my letters yet I would like to speak to you and tell you how good my mommy and daddy are. If you are busy please give a letter to the policeman whom I gave letter to on Sunday so he can give it to me.

Very Truly Yours,
Michael Rosenberg

Source: Dwight D. Eisenhower Presidential Library

Questions to guide the discussion of this letter include the following:

- How does history portray the Rosenbergs?

- How does this letter compare to history's portrayal?

- Consider how these events in history might be told from the perspectives of the following people or groups: the Rosenbergs themselves, their son, the United States government, U.S. citizens who support the death penalty, U.S. citizens who oppose the death penalty, and the Rosenbergs' friends and neighbors.

In another example, consider the following journal entry (Figure 5.8) written by Christopher Columbus in 1492. While this journal was not written by a child, it was written by someone familiar to students. Students can use this entry to think about Columbus's journey as if they were with Columbus himself. First, students can discuss Columbus's white lies (documenting fewer miles passed than actually traveled), and determine for themselves whether or not they think they are justified. Then, students can write journal entries of their own from the perspective of the sailors Columbus is talking to. Would they be hopeful? Despondent? Worried? Excited? Students can each choose a perspective and then justify it using what they learned about Columbus's voyage.

Figure 5.8—Journal of Columbus

Sunday, 9 September.

Sailed this day nineteen leagues, and determined to count less than the true number, that the crew might not be dismayed if the voyage should prove long. In the night sailed one hundred and twenty miles, at the rate of ten miles an hour, which make thirty leagues. The sailors steered badly, causing the vessels to fall to leeward toward the northeast, for which the Admiral reprimanded them repeatedly.

Source: Dwight D. Eisenhower Presidential Library

Using Signage to Teach Content

Signage includes documents categorized as posters, advertisements, and notices. These documents can sometimes be simpler to read and are therefore good entry-level primary sources for students to use. The texts vary in length, and sometimes they have pictures or illustrations to support the content. The document questions listed on page 96 can be easily applied with these documents.

Figure 5.9—Auction Broadside, 1829

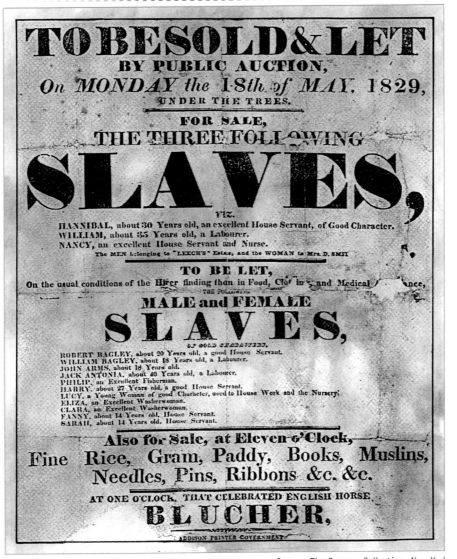

Questions to guide the discussion of signage include:

- Who is the intended audience?

- How do the symbols express a message?

- What is the author's purpose for creating this [poster, advertisement, notice]?

Consider the signage displayed in Figure 5.9. It helps students realize that slaves were real people. The signage also shows students that this auction would take place where people could buy food and sewing supplies. If the people waited around until the afternoon, they could even be entertained by a famous horse show. This document gives a very clear picture of the attitudes toward slaves during this time in history. As an instructional tool, students can discuss the kinds of events they might expect to see at modern-day fairs, flea markets, or farmer's markets, and compare these to the events advertised in this poster.

In a second example, middle school and high school students studying World Wars I and II may enjoy examining some propaganda posters (Figure 5.10) created by the United States government. For instructional purposes, students can discuss and determine the intents for the posters and whether or not they were effective. Students can also compare and contrast these war posters with one another or with those from other wars such as World War II, Vietnam, and the Cold War. After critical analysis, students can reflect on how propaganda posters have changed over time.

Figure 5.10—Propaganda Posters

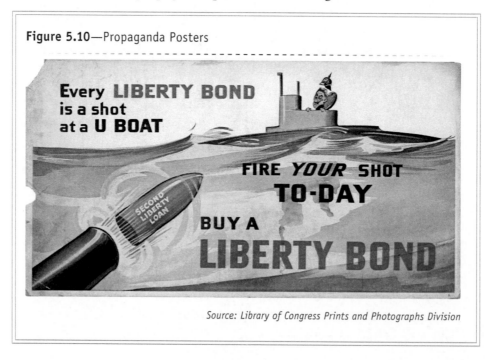

Source: Library of Congress Prints and Photographs Division

Figure 5.10 *(cont.)*

Source: Library of Congress Prints and Photographs Division

Using Maps to Teach Content

State or district curricula likely includes geography standards, some of which are related to the use and application of map reading. Using a variety of maps can help students practice map-reading skills as well as understand how geography is used to interpret the past. The following are three examples of how to use historical maps to address the application of map-reading skills and the learning and interpreting of history as well as the application of critical thinking through these skills.

Consider, for instance, John Smith's map of Virginia (Figure 5.11). It has many artistic details for students to analyze. Providing students with hand lenses will help them see details they may otherwise overlook. For students who may benefit from analyzing smaller portions at a time, divide the map into sections and assign certain sections to student groups. Then, students can collaborate to share their observations.

Figure 5.11—John Smith's Map of Virginia

Source: Library of Congress Rare Book and Special Collections Division

Sample questions to ask with this map or with others include:

- What is the title of the map?

- When was the map created?

- What type of map is it?

- Why was the map created?

- What is the scale of the map?

- Does it have a map key? What do the symbols represent?

- If it is a historic map, is it still accurate today?

- How does the map help you understand the period you are studying?

- What additional questions do you have?

- How does the picture relate to the map?

- What can we learn about the map through looking at the image?

Source: Library of Congress Prints and Photographs Division

At a first glance, students may think a child created the Map of Dachau (Figure 5.12). An effective strategy to start students thinking critically about a primary source is to have them make predictions about it, such as who made it, when, and why. Once students learn the history of this particular map, they will be surprised to learn that a medical army officer who helped liberate prisoners at Dachau drew it in 1945.

Figure 5.12—Map of Dachau

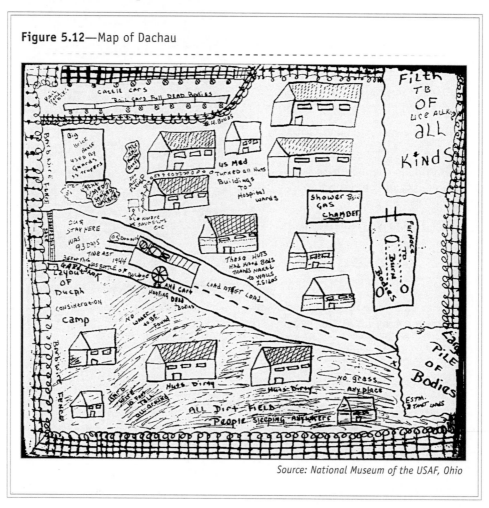

Source: National Museum of the USAF, Ohio

Aside from using maps to learn map-reading skills or to build historical knowledge, maps can also be used to help students learn to think critically. For example, the map of Bunker Hill (Figure 5.13), correctly named Breed's Hill shows the three hills on the peninsula of Charlestown. It was the site of a battle during the American Revolution. After analyzing the map's contents, students can work in small groups to come up with offensive battle plans if they were to attack the peninsula or defensive battle plans if they were to defend the peninsula. Following, students can learn the movements of both the American troops and the British troops during this battle, and compare their battle plan strategies with what really happened there.

Figure 5.13—The Battle of Bunker Hill

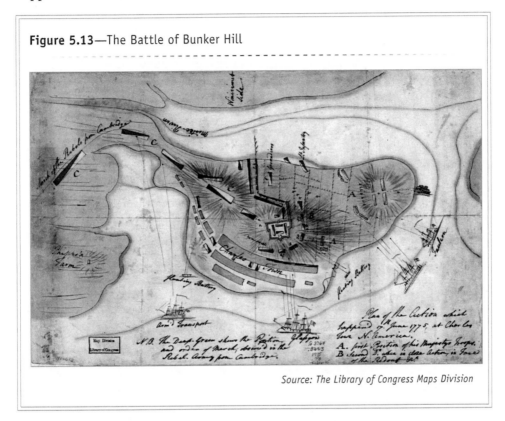

Source: The Library of Congress Maps Division

Using Cartoons to Teach Content

Political cartoons can be among the most challenging primary sources for students. They assume a great deal of background information of the reader, and they often have symbolism with which students may not be familiar. This requires high levels of evaluation and critical thinking on the part of students to learn from cartoons' content. Cartoons have very specific points of view. Authors create them to make points, influence the readers' opinions, persuade readers to accept another perspective, or ridicule people and events. When choosing a cartoon, consider what students need to know before understanding its message. Providing essential background knowledge will help students successfully interpret and make inferences from the cartoon's message, and understand the author's purpose for creating it.

Consider the example displayed in Figure 5.14. Students studying the causes of the American Revolution may view this cartoon. As students observe the people, setting, and actions, the questions can focus on the students' analyses of this cartoon and other cartoons. The questions range from basic to more complex. While upper-elementary students can begin to evaluate political cartoons, this level of questions is used more frequently as students move into middle and high school.

Figure 5.14—The Repeal, or Funeral Procession, of the Stamp Act

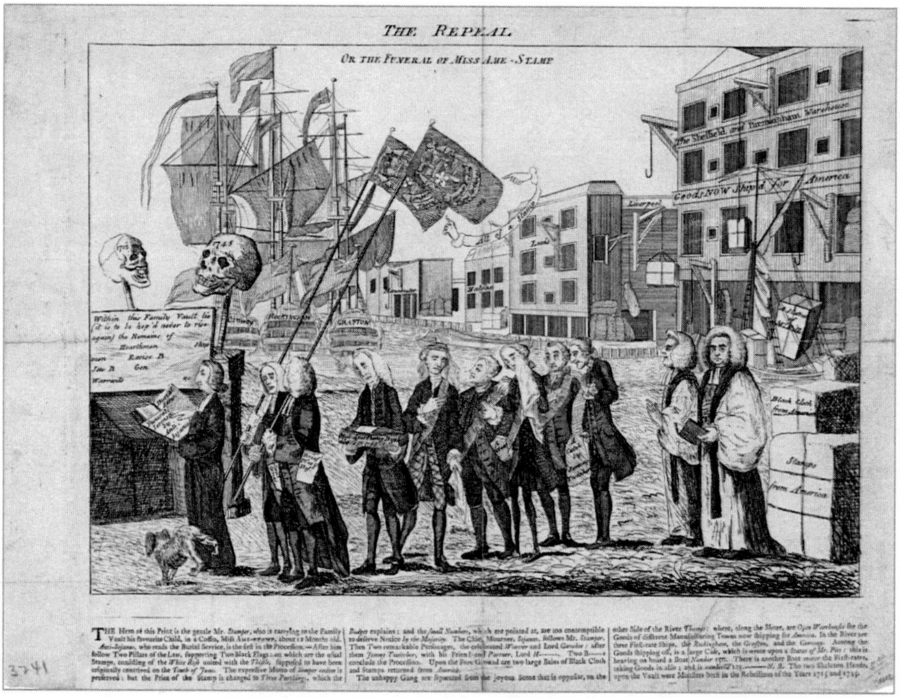

Source: Library of Congress Prints and Photographs Division

Sample questions to ask with this cartoon may include:

- What is the title or caption of the cartoon?

- What people and objects are in the cartoon?

- What words are in the cartoon?

- What are the symbols and what do they mean?

- Explain any exaggerations in the cartoon.

- What is the point of view of the cartoon?

- What is difficult to understand about the cartoon? Why?

- Do you agree or disagree with the point of view in the cartoon? Why?

- What are the cartoonist's political views?

The next cartoon (Figure 5.15) is related to the women's suffrage movement. At first glance, it looks simple and easy to understand. But it holds many hidden meanings that even older students may not grasp without instructional support, such as directing their attention to the way the two adults are dressed, asking them to draw inferences from their observations, or providing guiding questions such as the ones listed below the picture. (Note: Female students might say this cartoon is in favor of women's suffrage. Male students might say that it is against women's suffrage. Students should be brought to the realization that this cartoon offers varying viewpoints depending on the perspective of the reader.)

The Library of Congress Teaching with Primary Sources website (http://www.loc.gov/teachers/) has lesson plans and primary source collections with information for students in grades K through 12.

Figure 5.15—Election Day

Source: Library of Congress Prints and Photographs Division

Sample questions to ask with this cartoon may include:

- What time is it? Why is that important?
- Why are the babies crying?
- What do you notice about the cat's behavior?
- Is this cartoon for or against women's suffrage?

Document-Based Questioning

The use of primary sources in social studies provides students with an in-depth study of history from multiple perspectives and through a variety of media. Having these sources available is the first step toward an engaging study of a particular topic that is rich in content. Now, having analyzed documents with critical eyes, students need to do something with the information. One way students may demonstrate their understanding of content is through document-based questioning (DBQ), sometimes referred to as document-based assessment (DBA). This instructional strategy falls right in line with close reading. Whereas students read critically and analyze text with close reading, they interpret critically and analyze documents through the DBQ approach. According to Mollie Hackett (2013), this strategy supports reading skills and has added benefits for student learning. Since the texts, passages, and resources are generally shorter in length, they work well for modeling critical reading and thinking skills within the time constraints of a typical class period. When students work with such texts, they can put their mental energies into the analysis of the text rather than into the actual reading of the text. As students grow accustomed to thinking critically about what they are reading, they may apply these skills when reading longer passages, thus scaffolding their stamina for analyzing longer texts.

Essentially, DBQ is historical inquiry and document analysis. Students read and analyze a series of historical documents to respond in writing to a specific question, or to devise and compose a thoughtful thesis and/or argument all based on historical evidence. For obvious reasons, the DBQ instructional strategy is mostly designed to support student learning at the middle and high school levels, providing direct support for students taking Advanced Placement (AP) history exams. However, students in the elementary grades may begin to learn these analytical- and critical-thinking skills and apply them toward more simple writing assignments. This type of activity and instruction supports both the reading for information standards and writing standards.

From Document to Thesis

Providing opportunities for students to analyze documents is important, but it is only the first step in developing their understanding of history. Next, students should do something with the information to help them really learn it. This "something" usually amounts to some form of writing in response to reading, and a DBQ lesson is no different. With DBQs, the outcome is for students to respond to a specific question or to develop and support a thesis using evidence from the primary sources to justify their positions. This can be done in even the earliest grades, using primary sources suitable for the curriculum content at these levels. For example, students in kindergarten, first, or second grade may view photographs and then explain how communities have changed over time, or they may study several maps and compare the legends. Students in the upper-elementary grades may read letters and journals and then evaluate the level of commitment by soldiers of the Revolutionary War, or they may define regions of the United States by the culture of its people.

As students move into middle and high school, the analysis of the documents becomes more complex. Students use the documents to identify facts as well as opinions or interpretations. They should also look for bias in the documents. Students can identify those documents they consider most reliable and discuss the criteria they used for making those decisions. Additionally, their writing assignments become more complex. Assignments should require students to organize information in logical categories by analyzing the resources for content, perspective, and purpose. The expectation for students in these grades is that they write as historians—that is, as experts of a particular time period in history. The writing task requires students to take a position on a particular topic and use information provided from the primary sources as fuel to support and defend their position.

Consider a project designed by Mr. Martino, a high school teacher, in which students study primary sources from World War II and write reports on the use of atomic weapons. Along with the resources, Mr. Martino provided a series of three questions to help students focus their analyses and take notes about the content contained in the documents. As students responded to the questions, they sorted the documents into the following categories: military actions taken, reactions from soldiers or civilians, effects of atomic bombs, and information related to the future of warfare. Students then transformed the questions into focused thesis statements and used the information from their analyses to support their thesis statements.

Mr. Martino's questions for a DBQ thesis assignment related to the use of atomic weaponry:

- Was Truman justified in the use of atomic weaponry against Japan in WWII?

- How did the use of atomic weaponry impact the outcome of WWII?

- What are both positive and negative outcomes of the use of atomic weaponry during WWII?

Differentiating Instruction with Primary Sources

By using a series of diverse documents, you can effectively differentiate lessons. To support struggling students or English language learners, provide more visual documents than text documents. You can read complex documents aloud with students who need this instructional support either in small groups or by making a recording students can listen to as they follow along in the document. Not every student has to examine the same document; you can assign different ones to different groups that can then present their documents to the class. In this way, students can work with documents appropriate to their levels but they will still be exposed to other documents and learn content through the presentations and through whole-class discussions.

You can also differentiate the types of questions you ask about primary sources, assigning very focused questions to struggling students in ways that guide their comprehension and challenging advanced students with questions that require more analytical thought.

Chapter 5 Reflection

1. How can you help students understand the differences between primary and secondary sources?

2. Consider a unit that you will teach soon. How can you incorporate primary sources to provide students with a unique perspective of events?

3. What challenges do you expect when utilizing primary sources? How will you address them?

Chapter 6

Engaging Students in Research

Why do social scientists conduct research? Simply put, they want answers to questions they encounter when reading or thinking about their discipline. Why did Abraham Lincoln free the slaves only in the Southern states that had left the union? What would happen if electoral votes could be apportioned according to the popular vote in each state? What would have happened to the Roman Empire had Marius not reformed the Roman military? These are some of the questions that arise as social scientists study history and other social science disciplines.

Why should students conduct research? When students construct their own knowledge and answer questions that they find interesting, their efforts result in final products that convey their personal thinking rather than repetitions of others' ideas. One of the primary joys in learning is sharing new knowledge with someone else, particularly if it is something the student finds interesting or relevant to a current topic. The converging research on students conducting research concludes that learning starts with what the learner already knows. New knowledge must be connected to it and then constructed through experiencing and processing step by step, until higher level understanding is achieved (Smilkstein 2011).

Research reports also play key roles in the development of and application of students' writing skills as set forth in today's writing standards. These very clearly articulate that students should do the following:

- Write arguments to support claims of substantive topics or texts.

- Write informative/explanatory texts to examine and convey complex ideas.

- Conduct short as well as more sustained research projects.

- Gather relevant information from multiple print and digital sources.

- Draw evidence from informational texts to support analysis, reflection, and research.

Unfortunately, the typical history report, which usually boils down to a "born-did-died" summary of basic facts, is not engaging for most students—or their teachers! Students do little more with such projects than simply regurgitate information they read from books and online summaries. This outcome is not a model of actual research; it is more of a low-level comprehension task for students. They learn some facts that rarely extend beyond the remembering level of Bloom's Taxonomy (Figure 6.1).

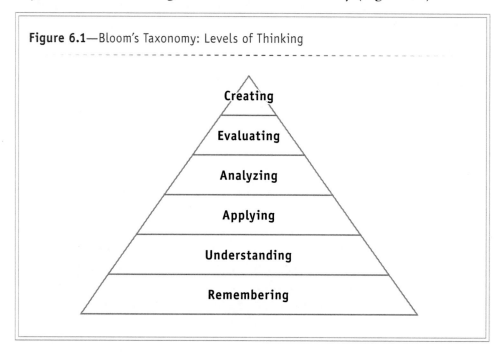

Figure 6.1—Bloom's Taxonomy: Levels of Thinking

Creating

Evaluating

Analyzing

Applying

Understanding

Remembering

For research to qualify as just that (research), the researcher should start with an open-ended question, the answer to which must be constructed by analyzing and synthesizing information from several sources. Robert Bain (2007) noted that historians start with a question, while teachers tend to start with the answer, the effects of which put the teacher in the center of learning and not the student. Therein lies the crux of the problem as to how to get students to write and think in nontraditional manners so that they may construct their own knowledge.

Teachers may believe that asking primary and intermediate elementary students to construct their own knowledge is beyond their cognitive abilities. However, studies show that it is not. The caveat is that teachers must teach or scaffold this level of knowledge in such a way as to allow students to practice constructing knowledge at appropriate cognitive levels.

For example, when studying American history, second or third grade students might be asked to answer *who*, *what*, *when*, and *where* questions about the content. These are important questions for students at these levels that are asked to ensure understanding of the basic facts about historical people and events. But teachers must move beyond these questions, also asking, "Why is this important to learn?" or "What is the significance of this information?" Students who are taught to think more deeply about content learn to apply critical-thinking skills, such as analyzing and evaluating, throughout their K–12 experiences. Authentic research projects are effective means of developing these thinking skills.

The following pages are intended to help you design purposeful research projects so that students read, comprehend, and think critically about informational text, synthesize facts and ideas thoughtfully, and present their newfound knowledge in meaningful ways.

Designing Meaningful Research Projects

A research project should excite and engage students, providing the motivation to do the challenging work necessary to answer interesting questions and present their learning effectively. Planning and teaching such a project involves several steps:

- Set a clear purpose and ask a compelling question.

- Determine a format.

- Provide assessment guidelines and a model project.

- Teach relevant research skills.

- Allow time for students to work through the research and writing process.

- Celebrate the results.

Each of these steps will be discussed in the following sections.

Set a Clear Purpose and Ask a Compelling Question

The first and most important step to assigning a research project is to have clear goals and learning targets that go beyond summarizing facts. Clarify your expectations, including objectives such as having students do the following:

- Develop supporting questions to guide research.

- Evaluate resources.

- Distinguish between key details and interesting ones.

- Write a compelling argument.

- Understand the contributions an individual or event made to the time.

After you've outlined your goals for students, it's time to develop a compelling question to guide students' research. For example, instead of assigning a traditional biography report about a person from history, ask, "Why is this person worth knowing about?" By refocusing the prompt just slightly, students will be less focused on the minor details of the person's life (such as when he or she was born and died) and more focused on two or three major accomplishments, such as those that spurred advancements in science, brought about societal changes, served their community, inspired others to reach new goals, taught others that one should never give up on his or her dreams, and so on. Now, students will be reading informational texts with a clear purpose in mind. They will need to sort through the unimportant facts and focus on details that show why the person is worth knowing.

Compelling research questions can arise in a variety of ways. Of course, you can develop your own to focus students on required content. But sometimes, questions emerge from students' natural curiosity about an event or a person encountered during the course of a unit. Other times, questions arise when students uncover contradictions in the available information about the event or topic (Marzano, Pickering, and Pollock 2012). Capitalize on these types of situations and use students' own questions to instigate an inquiry. As students investigate history, they will realize there are no quick, certain answers to their questions. This may frustrate students, but the drive to continue to find answers can be very motivating and engaging.

Other sources for generating questions for historical research are images and artifacts. When asked how she approaches a heretofore-unseen image, historian Jennifer Keene (2006) replied, "I start reading." She researches the background of the image, also known as metadata (when produced, by whom, where, etc.). Her goal is to contextualize the image so that when she studies it more closely, she understands as much as possible about why and how it came into being. For students who live in a world of images, beginning research with something visual or with tactile "hooks" gets them to start asking questions that use the full range of Bloom's continuum of thinking skills.

As you devise compelling questions, consider these prompts that require students to analyze and synthesize the facts they have learned for a greater purpose:

- What is the importance of learning about _____? (*event*)

- Why do we celebrate _____? (*holiday*)

- Why do we remember _____? (*notable person*)

- What did this person do that makes him or her notable?

- What does this _____ represent? (*symbol, flag, monument, etc.*)

- Why is this information important to our lives today?

Another consideration at this stage is how to incorporate choice. When students are able to choose their subject from within a topic, they are more likely to be engaged in the project and motivated to do quality work. This is especially true as students get older. For a biography project, you could provide a list of historical figures for students to choose from or allow them to choose their own person from a particular time frame. When studying the Industrial Revolution, each student can choose an invention to research, explaining how it came to be and how it affected society.

Determine the Format

Once you've outlined your objectives and have a clear purpose for research and a compelling question, consider the format in which you want students to present the results of their research. Often, projects will contain at least one writing component along with visuals, such as an informative essay with illustrations, a poster with an informational paragraph, or a how-to piece accompanied by a model. All or some of a project can be digital, incorporating audio, video, and/or graphic elements. Here are some examples of typical writing components of research projects:

- informational paragraph(s) or essay (such as the biography example in Figure 6.2)

- analytical paragraph(s) or essay (such as comparing and contrasting facts presented by two different authors or perspectives between first- and secondhand accounts of an event)

- argumentative paragraph(s) or essay (such as taking a position about a particular topic and using evidence and information to support the claim)

- reflective paragraph(s) or essay (such as summarizing lessons learned from a particular incident or event)

- expressive paragraph(s) or essay (such as explaining how past events apply to current situations, perhaps from a personal experience)

Students may write any one of several types of research reports:

- informational
- analytical
- argumentative
- reflective
- expressive

Figure 6.2—Student Example of a Biography Report

Laura Ingalls Wilder

Why is Laura Ingalls Wilder worth knowing about, you ask? Well, I'll tell you why. Laura inspired people to follow their dreams, and she wrote many great books that pleased kids. Still not impressed? Maybe you'll rethink that after you finish this essay.

First of all, Laura Ingalls Wilder inspired people to follow their dreams and not give up on themselves. How did she do it? She overcame the obstacles in her childhood. She had to move many times and to many different places. In 1874, Laura's dad built a spectacular house out of yellow pine boards, glass windows, and china doorknobs. But that summer, grasshoppers invaded the house, and Laura and her family had to move again! Even though she went through all those tough times, she managed to become a great author.

Second, Laura is an author worth knowing about. She wrote many great kid-friendly books that people of all ages adore. Laura liked to write about her childhood and her whole lifetime. She also wrote *Pioneer Girl* and *Little House in the Big Woods*, which sold millions of copies. It soon got rewritten into a television show.

Now, I bet you're convinced that Laura Ingalls Wilder is worth knowing about.

Provide Assessment Guidelines

Part of having a clear objective is knowing in advance how the assignment will be evaluated or graded. Completing a research project (or any creative writing task) without knowing how the project will be evaluated is kind of like shooting arrows at targets in the dark. The archer can be ready and fire, but the likelihood of hitting the target is lessened, because he doesn't know where to aim.

Evaluation criteria can take many forms, from simple checklists to detailed rubrics. Rating scales fall in between, having specific criteria similar to rubrics, such as *Project is organized*. But they leave room for more subjective scoring. The advantage to scales over rubrics is that they allow you to weigh some criteria more than others; for instance, you may decide that organization is worth just 10 percent of the overall score, while the content is weighted to total 50 percent of the overall score. Figures 6.3, 6.4, and 6.5 show various evaluation tools for a research project about local government, specifically how locally elected officials help serve the community in which they live. These examples illustrate how similar criteria can be weighted based on importance of content, organization, conventions, and quality of work.

Figure 6.3—Checklist for a Local Government Research Project

☑ Includes at least three locally elected positions

☑ Describes the roles of each of the three positions in detail

☑ Names the people who currently hold each of the three locally elected positions

☑ Explains how each of these individuals is involved in his or her community, citing specific examples (actions/events, locations, and how each action/event supports the community)

☑ Includes an introduction and a conclusion

☑ Uses correct grammar, spelling, and punctuation

☑ Is neat and well organized, and is an example of my best work

Total: _____ / 7

Figure 6.4—Two Different Rating Scales for a Local Government Research Project

Criteria	Value	Earned
Includes at least three locally elected positions	9	
Describes the role of each of the three positions in detail	15	
Names the people who currently hold each of the three locally elected positions	9	
Explains how each of these individuals is involved in the community, citing specific examples (actions/events, locations, and how each action/event supports the community)	45	
Includes an effective introduction and conclusion	6	
Uses correct grammar, spelling, and punctuation	6	
Is neat and well organized, and is an example of the student's best work	10	
Total	**100**	

Alternate scoring for the same project:

Criteria	Value	Earned
Includes at least three locally elected positions	5	
Describes the role of each of the three positions in detail using more than one reliable source for each	20	
Names the people who currently hold each of the three locally elected positions and who their opponent was in the most recent election	15	
Explains how each of these individuals is involved in the community, citing specific examples (actions/events, locations, and how each action/event supports the community)	40	
Includes an effective introduction and conclusion	10	
Uses correct grammar, spelling, and punctuation	5	
Is neat and well organized, and is an example of the student's best work	5	
Total	**100**	

Figure 6.5—Matrix Rubric

Category	4	3	2	1
Content	Includes at least three locally elected positions.	Includes two locally elected positions.	Includes one locally elected position.	Includes no locally elected positions.
	Thoroughly describes the role of each of the three positions in detail.	Satisfactorily describes the role of each position with some detail.	Describes the role of each position, but lacks detail.	Inaccurately describes the role of the positions mentioned.
	Correctly names the people who currently hold each of the three locally elected positions.	Correctly names two of the people who currently hold each locally elected position.	Correctly names one person who currently holds a locally elected position.	Incorrectly names the people who currently hold locally elected positions.
	Thoroughly explains how each of three locally elected individuals is involved in the community, citing specific examples and using explicit details.	Satisfactorily explains how each locally elected individual is involved in the community, citing examples and using details.	Explains how each locally elected individual is involved in the community, but lacks examples and details.	Does not explain how locally elected individuals are involved in the community.
Organization	Information is very organized with well-constructed paragraphs and subheadings.	Information is organized with well-constructed paragraphs.	Information lacks organization and/or paragraphs are not well constructed.	Information is disorganized, and paragraphs are not well constructed.
	Includes an effective introduction and conclusion.	Includes an effective introduction or conclusion.	Includes an introduction or conclusion that is ineffective.	Does not include an introduction and/or a conclusion.

Figure 6.5 *(cont.)*

Category	4	3	2	1
Conventions	Few or no grammatical, spelling, or punctuation errors.	Some grammatical, spelling, or punctuation errors.	Grammatical, spelling, or punctuation errors, and commonly used words are spelled incorrectly.	Many grammatical, spelling, or punctuation errors that interfere with the paper's fluidity.
Quality of Work	Is neat and visually appealing and is an example of the student's best work.	Is neat or visually appealing and is an example of the student's best work.	Is neat or visually appealing but is not an example of the student's best work.	Is not neat or well organized and is not an example of the student's best work.

Provide a Model

Students who want to do well on a project will likely ask numerous questions about the format, the expectations, the content, etc. Even students with some modicum of drive will inevitably ask, "How many pages does it have to be?" With a well-constructed evaluation tool, you can redirect students to use the criteria listed there to answer most of their questions. As for the length, some teachers like to limit students to a certain number of words or pages, but this is not recommended. Depending on the topic and assignment, some students may need three pages, whereas others may need eight to compose a thoughtful and complete response.

Another way to put students' minds at ease is to provide a model of the expectations. Think about how teachers go about writing a grant. Even having been given the criteria and having reviewed the evaluation tool, teachers want to see a winning example. This model helps us organize, compose, and complete our own grant to best meet the exacting expectations of the grant review committee. Students will do the same thing. They will use the example as a model for their own project. Providing a model will clearly illustrate the expectations set forth in the evaluation tool.

If this is the first time you have assigned this particular project, you will have to compose at least part of it yourself to demonstrate how the criteria should look on paper (or on screen). Be sure to save exemplary student work to use as models for subsequent school years, always asking students' permission before making copies to share with next year's class. Simply label a folder with the project name and "Student Models" and store it with your other project materials, and you'll be a step ahead next time. You can also scan work and store it in an electronic folder labeled by project name. Projects created digitally, such as in word-processing programs or online slide presentations, can be stored this way as well.

Teach Research Skills

At this point in the research project, students have clear visions and expectations for their report. Before they can write anything, however, they must do the research! This requires the use of informational resources, such as texts, articles, and primary sources. Students might also conduct interviews or listen to news broadcasts if these tasks fit into the scope of their topic. As they research, they will need to take notes and document sources, all of which are skills that need to be taught.

Gathering Sources

The age and ability of your students will determine the level of support you provide as they gather sources for research. Teachers may choose to support students in any of the following ways:

- Provide a selection of resources—including textbooks, informational books, reference materials, magazines, and digital resources—in the classroom for students to use.

- Ask the media specialist to identify and pull related resources and give students time to visit the library to review them.

- Allow students to search for resources themselves, using a select list of screened websites or a secure database, such as subscription-based EBSCO found in many school libraries.

In today's world, conducting some research online will enhance almost any research project. Internet safety is always a concern, so you'll want to preview all websites and limit students' ability to only search the sites you have approved. There are a few ways to do this. You can bookmark reliable sites and limit students to those. You can also create a web page with a list of links to approved websites. If you do not have a website, you can create a word-processing document and insert links to sites you wish students to use. This document can be transferred in any number of ways to the computers the students will be using, so they, too, have ready-access to the list. Both of these ideas eliminate students' frustration to find appropriate and useful websites by mistyping URLs or ending up at inappropriate, unreliable, or unusable websites.

Evaluating Print Sources

As students begin using sources, teach them how to evaluate materials both for their usefulness to the student and for the validity of information they may present. With younger students, focus on helping them determine if a particular resource contains the information they need by checking the table of contents and index. In addition, they should consider the text's reading level; if it is too high, the source will be of limited use to the student. In fifth grade and beyond, students can also consider the validity of the text by noting the qualifications of the author, the reputation of the journal or publisher, and the year of publication.

Evaluating Websites

Evaluating websites is of critical importance when using the Internet for research. It is a lifelong skill that students will take with them and apply in any number of contexts, both in and out of school. This can be a complex task, especially for young students who have difficulty distinguishing fiction from nonfiction, let alone a reliable website from an unreliable one. You can introduce this idea by informally discussing some of the criteria that follow as you bring students to sites for instructional purposes, leading students to understand that they should think critically about the sites they use for research. Upper elementary, middle, and high school teachers can use these criteria as part of a lesson or several lessons specifically related to teaching the differences between reliable and unreliable sources.

There are many lists of criteria, lesson plans, and worksheets related to teaching students about reliable web resources available. The criteria listed in Figure 6.6 were modified following the suggestions from the University of California, Berkeley (2012).

Figure 6.6—Criteria for Evaluating Websites for Reliability

What to Do	Questions to Ask
Read the URL information.	Is it a personal or commercial web page? Or, does it end with a reliable domain such as –.*gov*, –.*edu*, or –.*org*?
Scan the perimeter of the page.	Does it have a link to an "about us" or an "our philosophy" section or something similar? Is the page dated, and is the date current? Does it link to or include information about the authors?
Look for quality indicators.	Find embedded links such as "links," "additional sites," or "related links," etc. Investigate footnote references. Find copyright information.
Do further research.	Do an Internet search for the author(s). Look to make sure that the author has a reputation that can be trusted and that their published works are trustworthy.

Reading Informational Texts

Young students will likely need support to read and comprehend text-based research materials. These resources are likely written at readability levels above the students' independent reading levels. Informational texts tend to be more challenging because of the vocabulary and background knowledge they inherently expect from readers. (See chapter 3 for a full discussion of supporting students as they read informational texts.) During the research phase of a project, consider setting aside time to work with students individually or in small groups, or elicit assistance from willing parents or school-based volunteers to monitor comprehension, provide assistance, and answer questions as needed. Students who are just beginning to conduct research, struggling readers, and English language learners benefit from having a set of specific questions to answer as they read their texts. This scaffold helps them focus their attention on the important details and disregard extraneous facts that do not fit the research criteria.

Taking Notes and Documenting Sources

As students read, they should take notes on the relevant information they obtain from their sources. Chapter 4 has strategies for teaching note taking. For research purposes, it's imperative that students document the source from which the information comes. Using a simple note-taking sheet like the one shown in Figure 6.7 can prompt students to record the title, author, and year of the source. (A digital version of this chart is provided. See pages 205–206.) Older students will need to document the complete publication information and format it according to your preferred style, such as MLA or APA. In addition, be sure to teach students about paraphrasing and direct quotes, having them punctuate quotes properly and cite the page number on which a quotation occurs.

Figure 6.7—Note-Taking Template

My Research Topic:
Source Title:
Who wrote this?
What year was the source published?
Notes:

Allow Time for the Research and Writing Process

Report writing can be very time-consuming. Students need to have access to adequate resources, have time to read and gather information from them, organize the content of the information they gathered, and write and revise their work. With so little time to teach the content required by the standards, it can be difficult to find the time for students to work on their projects during class time. Integrating language arts and social studies instruction during a research project can help. Students can read for their project during independent reading time and work on the written component during writing workshop. Alternatively, these tasks may be assigned as homework. The challenge with this arrangement is that it can be hard to know who is doing the work: students, parents, or older siblings. English language learners and students with disabilities may struggle to complete lengthy projects independently. And students from impoverished homes have few resources available to attend to such a thorough project. To offset these obstacles, consider the following ideas:

- Have a wide range of reference materials for students to use in the classroom, all at varied readability levels.

- Schedule time to go to the computer lab. Or check out portable computers if students do not have individual access to online resources in the classroom or at home.

- Set aside 10 to 15 class minutes two or three times a week to allow students in-class time to work on their projects, and check in on their progress.

- Provide lunch-and-learn sessions during the school day where students meet with you during their lunch period to work on their projects.

- Provide before- or after-school sessions to assist students with their projects.

- Have a checklist of task completion items, and check in with students at the start of class to ensure that they are on pace to finish in time.

- Shorten students' assignment to include the bare minimum requirements.

Once students begin writing their essays, these same types of supports may be necessary to help all students succeed to the best of their abilities. Again, you can use class time to conference with students about the progress they are making, suggesting ways to improve the overall scope of the project. Parent volunteers can also help with this task. If students have been taught to conduct peer-conference reviews, students can help each other bring their projects to the next level.

Celebrate the Results

A research project requires investment of time and energy. Once it's complete, take time to celebrate the results. Having students share their projects with small groups, the whole class, or with a different class is a wonderful way to validate students' work and give them an authentic audience. If the project is large, inviting families in to hear presentations or view projects and chat with student authors can be a meaningful experience that strengthens the home-school connection. If the project is on a smaller scale or time is at a premium, consider displaying elements of the project on a class or hallway bulletin board.

"Doing" Oral History

For students of all ages, "doing" oral history presents unique and meaningful opportunities to conduct historical research. For younger students, it can begin with interviews of grandparents, parents, or others in their communities. The research conducted by middle and high school students in more formal oral history projects may have the potential to be used by other historians in a citation or to be published. Learning history by doing history is an effective and relevant way to get students involved in constructing their own learning.

The oral historian never undertakes an interview without having thoroughly researched his or her subject. The key to a successful oral history interview is a deep understanding of the context into which the subject's life fits. This depth of knowledge serves two very important purposes. First, it enables the interviewer to prepare substantive questions designed to elicit reflective and thoughtful responses from the subject of the history. Second, it allows the interviewer to ask "on the spot" follow-up questions that both probe and challenge the interviewee to remember in greater detail. A well-researched interviewer can offer information that clarifies the responses of the interviewee.

Good questions make for great answers. In the case of doing oral history, having good questions is a prerequisite to an interview that will serve as a valuable primary source for study now and in the future. Understanding how to develop open-ended questions and the ability to use follow-up questions that clarify are important skills for students doing oral history and beyond.

Examples of open-ended questions for oral history are:

• Who is the person who had the greatest impact on your life?

• What leader do you admire the most, and why?

• What are some of the most difficult choices you've had to make, and what made them difficult?

• What do you hope to leave behind after you are gone?

Numerous print resources exist that delineate the steps for planning, organizing, implementing, and managing oral history projects. Two sources are *The Oral History Manual* by Barbara W. Sommer and Mary Kay Quinlan and the Oral History Association website (http://www.oralhistory.org). There are also regional organizations that fall under the auspices of the American Association for State and Local History. The Library of Congress's Oral History Interviews is viewable online and has helpful ideas for involving students in doing oral history.

Teaching Students to Use the Internet Responsibly

Chances are, students in today's classrooms are more than capable of conducting simple online searches related to various topics of interest. As stated earlier, if students are left to their own devices, they may end up simply copying and pasting information into text documents and calling it done. It is becoming increasingly important to educate students about not only how to access information on the Internet but how to evaluate the sources they use as well. Teachers and students need to apply historical thinking skills to the way that they look at sources found on the Internet. These historical thinking skills involve the same practices that a historian would use when questioning the validity of an artifact that has been discovered. Each source needs to be evaluated from a number of different perspectives before it can be trusted. "Reliable information is to civic intelligence what clean air and clean water are to public health" (Wineburg 2016).

Students need clear understandings of what is expected of them when they are online or using technology to complete schoolwork. The International Society of Technology Education (ISTE) has outlined a set of National Education Technology Standards for students (NETS-S). According to the ISTE website, "simply being able to use technology is no longer enough. Today's students need to be able to use technology to analyze, learn, and explore. Digital age skills are vital for preparing students to work, live, and contribute to the social and civic fabric of their communities." The six NETS-S categories and their overarching statements are shown in Figure 6.8. What teachers should understand from these standards is that students need to be taught to use technology responsibly. They must also understand how to distinguish reliable websites from unreliable websites. Teachers should talk with their students before beginning a research project about the importance of doing their own work and not just copying information they think looks or sounds good. Students need to realize that the web represents only one venue for research.

Figure 6.8—ISTE NETS-S Standards and Anchor Statements

Standard	Anchor Statement
Creativity and Innovation	Students demonstrate creative thinking, construct knowledge, and develop innovative products and processes using technology.
Communication and Collaboration	Students use digital media and environments to communicate and work collaboratively, including at a distance, to support individual learning and contribute to the learning of others.
Research and Information Literacy	Students apply digital tools to gather, evaluate, and use information.
Critical Thinking, Problem Solving, and Decision Making	Students use critical-thinking skills to plan and conduct research, manage projects, solve problems, and make informed decisions using appropriate digital tools and resources.
Digital Citizenship	Students understand human, cultural, and societal issues related to technology and practice legal and ethical behavior.
Technology Operations	Students demonstrate a sound understanding of technology concepts, systems, and operations.

Chapter 6 Reflection

1. Think about a research project you have had your students undertake in your classroom. How might you adapt it to elicit higher levels of thinking?

2. How might you incorporate more time for student research in your already overloaded curriculum?

3. Which of the ideas discussed in this chapter will you implement in your teaching?

4. How can you best support students as they undertake independent research projects?

Chapter 7

Hands-On Strategies and Simulations

When adults think back about what they remember most about social studies, they often describe hands-on activities, interactive simulations, or culminating unit activities. These experiences, ones in which they were active participants, often become part of the lasting memories of students—along with the information learned while participating in them. "Research is now validating what teachers have known intuitively all along: hands-on learning increases retention and understanding" (Sundem and Pikiewicz 2005, 4). These activities provide opportunities for students to touch objects, make observations, ask questions, and draw logical inferences. Participating in simulations or role-playing enables them to feel as if they have personally participated in a historical event, perhaps from the perspective of an important historical figure. These experiences allow students to view history from various perspectives, allowing them to better understand the motives of individuals and the outcomes of their actions.

This chapter examines a number of hands-on strategies, as well as simulations that help students become active, engaged participants in history.

Using Realia (Objects) to Tell History

Objects, sometimes referred to as realia, offer insights into the everyday life of people from a particular culture, and they can make history tangible to present-day students. To help students understand the power of analyzing objects to learn about the past, first invite them to become archaeologists of the future, using objects from their own lives to tell tomorrow's history. Provide small groups of students with a common object such as a fast-food restaurant cup, a baseball cap with a national team logo, a ballpoint pen, a digital watch, or an old shoe, etc. Tell them that archaeologists examine artifacts carefully to learn about the society that made and used them.

Ask students to pretend to be archaeologists living 2,000 years from now who have recently discovered these artifacts. Have students make observations by describing what they see (form, material, pattern, words, colors, etc.). Then, have students make inferences about the items and the society in which they were used by asking questions such as the following:

- Who made it?

- Who might have used it?

- How was it used?

- What do you notice about the designs or motifs?

- What can we learn about the time period in which it was made?

Another engaging activity that demonstrates how to learn from artifacts involves students bringing in two or three items from home that best represent them. (If something is too large or impractical to bring in, a photo or a drawing can be substituted.) Baseball cards, ribbons, or a set of paints, for example, provide insight into students' hobbies and interests. On the day of the activity, tell students they will be participating in an anthropological study, and ask them to set their objects on their desks. Give each student a recording sheet. (See example in Figure 7.1.) (A digital version of this chart is provided. See pages 205–206.) Explain that they will circulate through the classroom, choosing three to five sets of objects to study. For each set, have students record detailed observations about each object, and then make inferences about the owner based on the object. After 10 to 15 minutes of recording, have each student present the object(s) he or she brought in. Students who studied those objects will compare the actual information with the inferences they wrote down to see if their observations were enough to make accurate inferences. Following this activity, the class can discuss the advantages and disadvantages of using objects to inform them about people, places, and events of the past.

Once students have experience using objects to make inferences and to "tell a story" about the people who used them, you can introduce an object related to a historical unit of study. The question stems in Figure 7.2 can guide students' analyses of the object, or you can use the Artifact Analysis Worksheet from the National Archives and Records Administration website (http://www.archives.gov/; search for "artifact analysis worksheet"). These sheets provide questions to help students focus their examination of an object, guiding them to note observable characteristics and make inferences from the artifact. Or students can record their observations and inferences on two-column charts, such as this one.

Figure 7.1—Chart to Record Observations and Inferences

Observations	Inferences

Figure 7.2—Question Stems for Studying Artifacts

- What do you think it is made of (e.g., bone, pottery, wood, metal, leather, plastic)?
- How does it look and feel (e.g., shape, color, texture, weight, any print)?
- What do you think it was used for?
- Who might have used it?
- Who do you think made it?
- What do you notice about the designs (or motifs)?
- Are there any interesting words or phrases on the artifact? Can you tell what language they're in?
- What can we learn about the people who made or used this object?
- Were the people rich or poor? Why do you think that?
- Is the object really old? Or was it made recently? Why do you think that?
- Is this a one-of-a-kind artifact, or are there many just like it?
- What can we learn about the time period in which it was made?
- What object do we have today that is similar to this object?

Locating Artifacts

You can often find objects for study at flea markets and antique stores. Museums or living-history sites might also have replicas of objects for purchase. Colonial Williamsburg, for instance, has an array of toys, children's games, and colonial money. Through their catalogue, you can purchase artifact "kits" such as items that would be found in a slave's bag or in a woman's pocket. Colonial Williamsburg also sells a simulation kit titled "Discovering the Past through Archaeology: A Classroom Simulation," which contains reproductions of artifacts, primary documents and instructions for creating an excavation site in the classroom. Check with their local museums and historical sites to see if they lend out historical artifact boxes or trunks. Some "traveling trunks" may require a nominal rental fee.

If actual artifacts are unavailable, head online to find images of objects you would like students to explore. Also consider using postcards, posters, photographs, or any other visual to give students a sense of the object. For example, students looking at a postcard of George Washington's fan chair can record observations about it and then infer why this chair was important to George Washington.

What's in Your Pocket?

Similar to the personal anthropological study described on page 134, you can present an activity called "What's In Your Pocket?," adapted from a lesson posted on the Library of Congress Teaching with Primary Sources website (http://www.loc.gov/teachers). Pair students with partners with whom they do not usually interact and explain the process: The first student describes something in his or her pocket, purse, or book bag. The second student asks questions about it. Then, the second student hypothesizes about what the item tells about the first student; the students discuss whether or not the hypothesis is correct. Students then switch roles so that each has the opportunity to hypothesize what can be learned from an object.

Extend this idea to make historical figures more accessible for students. For example, students studying the Civil War can examine the objects that were in Abraham Lincoln's pockets on April 14, 1865. These items are displayed on the Library of Congress America's Story site (http://www.americaslibrary.gov). While ordinary objects such as glasses and a wallet were in his pocket, students will likely enjoy surmising why he also carried a $5 Confederate note. You can also use this idea to study characters in historical fiction. For example, after reading *Johnny Tremain* by Esther Forbes, students can think about what would be in the pocket of the apprentice (Johnny Tremain), the merchant (John Hancock), a master craftsman (Paul Revere), or one of the female characters (Priscilla Lapham, Miss Lavinia, or Mrs. Bessie). Then, students can recreate their character's pocket(s) and justify each item they include in written summaries.

Another extension of the "What's in Your Pocket?" activity is gathering and creating objects for a fanny pack. This engaging activity is from Professor Dennis Dennenberg, retired from Millersville University. At the conclusion of a biography unit or a unit on heroes, or after students have thoroughly researched the accomplishments of a notable individual, they each create a fanny pack of object replicas, pictures or documents that provide significant information about a person's life. Rather than writing reports, students assemble items to be placed in fanny packs. Individual students present their packs to their classmates and reveal one item at a time, being prepared to justify the inclusion of each object. Classmates in the audience try to guess the individual represented by the objects. A sample pack for George Washington Carver might include the following:

- peanuts (Carver discovered over 300 uses for the peanut.)

- cotton (Cotton crops depleted the soil, so Carver sought ways to diversify crops.)

- soybeans (Carver invented a process for producing paints and stains from soybeans.)

- test tube (This was one of Carver's "tools" in the laboratory.)

- quote: "Education is the key to unlock the golden door of freedom."

- white flower (Carver always had one in his lapel pocket.)

- picture of a piano (He loved playing the piano.)

- picture of Carver with the faculty at Tuskegee University

Building Experiences through Field Trips

Field trips enable students to expand their learning beyond the classroom. They provide students with experiences that cannot be recreated in the classroom but are nevertheless aligned with instructional objectives, allowing students to acquire information through active hands-on experiences that deepen their understanding of a topic. To prepare for a trip, discuss with students the purpose of the trip, and provide any needed background knowledge ahead of time. This includes introducing vocabulary, displaying and discussing pictures, or providing time to explore the destination's website. Students should also begin developing questions about the destination as well as discussing examples of good questions for tour guides, docents, or re-enactors at the site.

Depending on the purpose and type of trip, students might bring notebooks, journals, or sketchpads to record information. You might also provide a scavenger hunt activity if the site does not have guides; having a list of exhibits to check out ensures students will see the most relevant parts of the site. During the trip, students need time to observe, ask questions, and talk about what they see and experience. After the trip, allow time for students to reflect on their experiences:

- Provide time for students to make general observations and reactions.

- Ask students to compare the hands-on experience with what they have already learned.

- Have students evaluate the most important display or object that they observed.

- Create a classroom display of pictures, literature, and items students collected.

- Give students an authentic summary activity, such as writing thank-you letters describing what they liked best about the trip and what they learned or having them write an article for the school newspaper.

Building Classroom Museums

Students can also create their own museum exhibits. This authentic activity is often used as a culminating project. Prior to the project, students should visit a museum and discuss the work of curators and people who are responsible for displaying artifacts. Students should consider how objects are shown, examine the labels on the objects, note the descriptive information on the walls/placards, and, if possible, talk or chat with (or email) a curator or exhibit designer to ask clarifying questions about setting up an exhibit.

Then, working individually or in small groups, students can create objects as part of the culture or time period under study and design museum displays. For example, if a class is concluding a study of ancient China, each student would select a topic and an object from the society that interests them. Students would then research the objects using some of the questions previously discussed (pages 134–135) and examine the use or impact of each one on Chinese society. Creating a model of the actual object can be done in class or as a homework assignment. Using actual museum labels as examples, students write short labels for their objects including:

- object's name

- its composition

- its owner

- its use and importance in the society

As part of this project, you can assign an additional piece of written text about the object to be included in the museum's catalogue, such as interesting facts or a time line of events surrounding the object's importance. Be sure to develop clear parameters for the assignment and share them with students, perhaps in the form of a checklist or rubric. Providing a model display is also helpful. When the museum is completed, invite parents and other visitors to the classroom to see the displays. Students act as curators and explain their parts of the exhibition using additional information from their research to elaborate on their artifacts.

This activity has the added benefit of being an interdisciplinary project. Students begin by picking topics in which they are interested. They use critical- and creative-thinking skills to research and design their objects.

The labels and written text for the catalogue require them to utilize writing skills, and finally, they practice speaking and listening skills when families and friends tour the museum and ask them questions. Throughout this process, students begin thinking like historians and museum curators.

The Smithsonian Education site (http://www.smithsonianeducation.org) provides a more in depth explanation of how to create classroom museums; search for "classroom museum" on the site for lesson plans and activities.

Going Places with Internet Resources

Financial resources limit the number of field trips schools can offer, and some places are impossible to visit. Virtual or electronic field trips are an effective alternative. These trips are interactive and can be repeated often. An added benefit is that students can move through them at their own pace. One example of this is a virtual visit to the Tenement Museum in New York City (http://www.tenement.org/tours.php). Students listen to an audio tour with the reading of primary sources as they "walk through" each family's apartment in the tenement. Many history sites now include virtual tours on their websites.

The National Park Service has a website entitled Teaching with Historic Places (http://www.nps.gov/subjects/teachingwithhistoricplaces/index.htm). Materials provided on this website enable students to learn about places without leaving their classrooms. Lesson plans guide students to examine and question readings, documents, maps, and photographs. Each lesson begins with an inquiry question, and the activities enable students to connect these historic sites to the broad themes of American history. For instance, the materials in the lesson plan on Thomas Edison's Laboratories in West Orange, New Jersey, include readings and images. All the activities lead students to consider the process of invention and its impact on society.

Exploring Places with Hands-on Geography

Geography is best learned by actually traveling to places around the county, around the state, around the nation, and around the world. Unfortunately, no school can offer these types of experiences on a regular basis. However, hands-on and online resources provide viable options for building geography knowledge.

To teach students about the geography of an area or a region, first provide them with a diversity of geographic information to build background knowledge for further in-depth study. Gather a wide variety of geographic information and give collaborative groups of students ample time to examine it. Students need to have experiences with the tools of a geographer, so have them observe and analyze a variety of maps, including physical and political, rainfall and vegetation, topographic, population-density, and transportation-and-trade-network maps. Also give students the opportunity to review geographic databases containing land-use information or crop-production levels, satellite images, and aerial photographs. While students will work with all this geographic information later in the unit in greater detail, an initial examination helps generate interest and often sparks conversations about similarities and differences among the maps themselves and information they hold. When students have had time to examine the resources, you can have them develop a KWHL chart as a way of compiling information and generating questions to drive instruction. This variation of the KWL Chart (page 34) adds an important step: the *H* refers to *how* students will find the information they want to know, encouraging them to think about what types of sources would be relevant. As the unit progresses, students complete the last section of the chart, listing what they have learned (*L*).

To add a level of critical thinking, trim the maps you provide in such a way that students cannot identify the specific region or part of the world they are to study. In this case, do not tell students the name of the region. Instead, have them use clues from the maps to hypothesize as to what part of the world they will study. At the end of the initial investigation of geographic resources, reveal the region to the students and review their ideas, modeling deductive-reasoning skills.

Engaging Students with Simulations

Simulations are real-life or experiential role-plays, so to speak, in which students make decisions within a specific context and then experience the outcomes of their decisions. Simulations are not free play. This game-like learning strategy is designed with a particular objective. For example, a simulation involving students in a mock congressional hearing might help students better understand how government works. Simulations are also very engaging to students. In an ideal simulation, every student has a role, and everyone is equally as involved as everyone else. Some simulations are quick and easy to implement; others can require quite a bit of prep-work and instructional time to "play out." Even so, most simulations are easily adaptable to meet the needs of the students and the classroom. They may be modified by the amount of time they take, the roles students play, and the manner in which students are evaluated.

Simulations used to be experienced live only in the classroom. However, in the digital age, many software and online simulations now offer students a wide variety of games and activities that simulate real events across all areas of the social studies. They are easily accessible to anyone with a computer and Internet access. Although students tend to gravitate toward anything electronic, to ensure that students are meeting the learning objectives when they use online simulations, follow up with class discussions, written reflections, or some other manner of holding students accountable for their learning.

Many teachers have discovered the value of using simulations as part of a comprehensive social studies course of study. Even Harvard business professors use simulations to build deeper understanding of the concepts they teach. In an online article by Harvard Business Publishing, Harvard professors shared their experiences with using simulations (or "sims," as they call them), stating that they "challenge students to analyze available information and make critical decisions to solve a [challenge]" (2015, 1). They also conclude that the best simulations allow students to experiment with ideas and outcomes and ultimately master the application of concepts to real situations. What could possibly support the development of twenty-first century thinking skills more than that? The following pages offer ideas and suggestions to use simulations to support concept development as well as to demonstrate events in history through the eyes of those who were there.

Remember to include the use of Google Maps™ and Google Earth™! Students can access information about locations, distance, elevation, geographical features, landmarks, and a host of other geographic topics using either or both of these resources. To see what's out there (literally!), simply search for Google Maps™ or Google Earth™ in the Classroom.

Simulations to Learn Concepts

Concepts are the over-arching topics around which a lesson or a unit is built. For example, primary students may learn economic concepts such as wants, needs, barter, trade, producers, and consumers. They may also learn about supply and demand, scarcity, opportunity costs, interdependence, specialization, resources (including natural, capital, and human), and goods and services. These concepts may not pose quite as much of a challenge to learn because students likely have personal experiences that enable them to make connections with their own lives. As students learn about these concepts, they should know and be able to use the terminology they learn in new situations.

To use a simulation to support the development of these primary-level concepts, you can use an online resource to demonstrate the differences between wants and needs. One game from PBS Kids Go! titled Mad Money (http://pbskids.org/itsmylife/games/mad_money_flash.html) has students choose a "big ticket" item for which they are to save money as they earn, save, and spend their way through thirty days of real-life situations. Online simulations have the advantage of being displayed for the whole class to experience at one time. They become even more engaging with the use of an interactive whiteboard. Or you can assign students to conduct the simulation at individual student computer stations. If every student does not have a computer, the class can rotate through the simulation or students can work with a partner at each individual student station. Regardless of the delivery method, ensure learning has happened by having students respond to a simple question, record their learning in their journals, or follow up with a more detailed writing assignment, such as writing a story about a boy or a girl who wants to save money for a special purchase and the process he or she goes through to accomplish the objective.

You can also use published resources that have students role-play situations in which they must make economic choices based on the concepts listed. One such resource is *Saturday Market* by Patricia Grossman and Enrique O. Sanchez. After reading the book aloud and discussing economic concepts, each student acts as a producer of a good or a service as well as a consumer. The class enacts a market day simulation, buying and selling goods and services. After a class discussion of the activity, students can record their experiences in learning journals, using specific terms related to this unit of study.

To find online simulation activities, conduct an Internet search using the concept's key word(s): *simulation*, and *for students*. For example, to find a simulation related to the three branches of the United States government, search using these words: *government simulation for kids*.

Simulations to Experience Events

Simulations can also allow students to become active participants in events from history. For example, to understand the conditions and challenges the colonists faced when journeying to Jamestown, students can role-play individuals on the Susan Constant under the leadership of the captain, Christopher Newport. Here is how this particular simulation might run.

Susan Constant Simulation

Begin by blocking off a section of the classroom floor for the boat. The boat was actually a little bigger than a school bus. Discuss with students the reasons men went to Jamestown in 1607. Assign students roles such as Reverend Robert Hunt, John Smith, carpenters, crewmembers, one of the boys, and the gentlemen. Give students paper bags, and tell them they can each bring one thing for the journey. Have them describe the item or draw a picture to put in the sack. To begin the simulation, students board the ship via "a gangplank" and sit on the floor of the boat. Explain that they are sitting in the hold of the ship. Only the crew and boys can come onto the deck. Take on the role of Christopher Newport and retell the experience. Include factual details such as the departure day (December 20, 1606), that there was no wind so the ships were stuck in the English Channel for six weeks, and that they did not actually get underway until February. Have students sway back and forth to simulate the movement of the boat. Discuss hunger, mice, and rats on the ship, crowded conditions, boredom, sickness, and storms. Provide a sample of hardtack. Explain how people on the ship (other than crew members) passed the days. Allow students a brief stretch when the ship stops to pick up supplies in the Canary Islands and the West Indies. When students arrive at the Chesapeake Bay, have students wait to leave ship (another two weeks) until a good harbor site is found. Before leaving the boat, also discuss where people will sleep and what they will eat. Open the bags, and see if students can use anything they brought with them.

As with any simulation, debriefing the activity is essential. In this example, students should discuss their feelings during the voyage and when land is finally sighted, why there were no women, different roles of individuals, and space issues. Students should also individually process the information by writing journal entries or sending letters back to their families in England describing their experiences and their emotional states. An online version of this activity is available on the Kids and History website (http://www.kidsandhistory.net).

Don't forget the apps! Students can play social studies-related games any time on any device using game-like apps. One example is "Stack the States" available for both Android™ and Apple®.

Some simulations are game-like in nature. For example, middle and high school students might participate in a game called "Feudal Candy." (This activity is available at http://www.classroomzoom.com/lessons/386/simulation-feudal-candy.) The objective of the activity is to help students identify the order of societal rank and loyalties within feudal Europe. Students take on the roles of the king, nobles, vassals, and peasants; small candy pieces represent the harvest. (Other items, such as pencils and stickers, can be substituted for candy.) Distribute the candy to the peasants. The vassals confiscate six candies from each peasant. From each peasant's payment, the vassal keeps one candy and gives five to his noble. The noble, in turn, takes two pieces of each vassal's payment and gives the remaining three to the king. At the conclusion of the activity, the students discuss the problems faced by the peasants, the power of the king and nobles, and the feudal system's power structure. They can also compare this system to today's Constitutional Republic, making connections and identifying similarities and differences between the two systems.

Speaking of which, this activity can also be adapted for American history students to learn the impact of taxation and underlying economic causes of the Revolutionary War. (This activity titled, "We the People: A History," is available at Discovery Education online, http://www.discoveryeducation.com/teachers/free-lesson-plans/we-the-people-a-history.cfm.) First, brainstorm a list of taxes that can be imposed on common classroom items and activities, such as writing with a pencil or not sitting up straight; specify how many pieces of candy must be paid for each tax. Compile 10 to 12 taxes, and display on the board. Then, give students role identification cards: King George III (1), members of Parliament (2), tax collector (2), and colonist (for everyone else). Distribute the candy (or other chosen item) to the colonists. Explain that the tax collectors will collect the taxes from the colonists. Determine how long to let the tax collection period run. When the time comes to send taxes to Parliament, gather all the tax collected. Demonstrate that half of the tax goes to the king, and three-quarters of the remaining amount is divided among the members of Parliament. The tax collectors keep what is left (one eighth of the total). Then, hold a discussion about how students felt during the process, helping students understand the concept of "no taxation without representation."

Both activities in this section were adapted from lessons created by two teachers from Bath County, Virginia.

Service Learning Experiences

Perhaps the most common problem-based learning is service learning. Many schools nationwide have made service learning a part of their graduation requirements for students. Teachers should be cautious to make the distinction between service learning and community service.

- Service learning focuses on students learning a process for activism in the community that requires a great deal of research and knowledge about the issue or topic under study in the classroom.

- Community service focuses on involvement in the community through volunteerism and is often extraneous to the curriculum being taught during the school day.

Both types of community involvement have purpose, value, and a place in schools, but service learning in particular will engage students in problem based learning. There are two outstanding models for teaching the processes of service learning that are solid, well-researched, and documented in terms of their success in changing students' attitudes toward civic involvement as well as deeply immersing them in a study of a current school, community, or state issue. Both of these programs are geared toward upper-elementary, middle, and high school students.

Active Citizenship Today (ACT)

Active Citizenship Today of the Constitutional Rights Foundation is recommended for the middle and high school levels. Written in an accessible manner for students, it outlines a process for identifying an issue or concern to the community and taking action. The five-step process includes:

- Where Do You Live? Looking at Your Community

- What's the Problem? Focusing on an Issue

- Who's Doing What? Searching for Solutions

- What Can You Do? Exploring Options

- What Will You Do? Taking Action

Source: Constitutional Rights Foundation

We the People: Project Citizen

The Project Citizen (PC) program is developed by the Center for Civic Education and has in many ways a similar framework to that of ACT's. It teaches students a process for researching the public policy related to an issue and asks them to offer an alternative solution to the problem. The difference in the two programs is that PC culminates with students participating in a competition where they present their issues and solutions to a group of adult judges, one of whom is an expert in a field related to the chosen topic, with the option of taking action.

The PC process includes:

- Introduction to public policy

- Identifying problems to be dealt with by public policy

- Selecting a problem(s) for your class to study

- Gathering information about the problem you will study

- Organizing the information you have gathered

- Developing a portfolio to present your research

- Presenting your portfolio in a simulated public hearing

- Reflecting on your experience: Why is citizen participation important to democracy?

Source: Center for Civic Education

Case Studies

Case studies are effective problem-based strategies. Case studies pose a problem from history for students to discuss and solve. A key part of the case study is the inclusion of primary-source material. The teacher prepares the case study for students and distributes copies of the problem as well as the supporting primary-source material. The following steps are most helpful in creating case studies for your students.

- **Step 1: Clarify objectives**—What does the teacher want students to learn from the discussion of the case? What do the students know already that applies to the case? What are the issues (central and peripheral) that may be raised in discussion? Can the case "carry" the discussion? Is it appropriate to your objectives?

- **Step 2: Plan and prepare**—How will the case and discussion be introduced? What preparation is required for students? (Written summaries and reaction papers? Analyses and discussion skills?) What question(s) will open the discussion? How will class time be appropriated for the issues to be discussed? Which concepts will be applied or extracted from the discussion? How will the discussion be concluded? How will students evaluate their own participation in the discussion? How will the teacher evaluate the participants?

- **Step 3: Consider what's going on**—What are the perspectives of the historical figures involved in this case study? What are the relationships among the historical figures? What is the chronology of events? What, in particular, is the perspective of the protagonist, the decision maker?

- **Step 4: Analysis of the case**—What is the central problem, the decision to be made? What are the issues? What theories or concepts are applicable to the situation presented? How can students be organically led to this line of thinking?

- **Step 5: Actions to be taken**—What is the variety of possible solutions to the problem presented? How will historical evidence and conceptual support for the proposed solutions be used? How will the proposed solutions be evaluated in light of their historical context? Is there an alternative, a "Plan B," just in case there is a need for one?

- **Step 6: Evaluation**—How will the content knowledge of the case, the contribution of each student to the discussion and group work, and the historical relevance and quality of the solution presented be evaluated?

The Boston Tea Party can be an example of a case study. In planning and preparing for this case study, a teacher would want to include the economic, political, and social issues that existed prior to the event. As the teacher summarizes the information for the case study, he or she needs to be sure to balance the information given to students presenting both the British and colonial points of view. Including excerpts from written documents, images, and charts adds to your ability to present an engaging, well-rounded portrayal of the case. The teacher will also want to cite the sources used, both primary and secondary, including page numbers for students who may wish to further investigate the case.

Tadahisa Kuroda, history professor emeritus from Skidmore College, has perfected the use of case studies. He recommends that students be given the case-study packet prior to the discussion in class and come prepared with a one-to-two-page summary of the points they wish to make regarding the case study. When the case study is completed, Dr. Kuroda has a variety of assessment questions he asks of his students. Among them are *What is the most important thing you learned from other students? What is the most important thing you offered to other students? How did the content from the case study apply to either what is being studied in class or to your own life?* These questions encourage students to value the thinking of their classmates and appreciate what can be learned from others.

Case studies can be produced by the teacher from scratch or adapted from other sources. Three sources in particular that lend themselves to this kind of adaptation are *After the Fact: The Art of Historical Detection* by James West Davidson and Mark Hamilton Lytle, *American Experiences* by Randy J. Roberts and James S. Olson, and *Teaching U.S. History as Mystery* by David Gerwin and Jack Zevin. A number of sources are also available that present both sides of an issue that are helpful in designing a case study exercise.

Students must do more than merely conduct research on their study. The facts that they gather only become useful if they can be organized into an easily accessible and usable form. Published resources provide a range of social-studies-writing strategies, including a variety of graphic organizers. One example is *Strategies for Writing in the Social Studies Classroom* by Kathleen Kopp. The strategies and graphic organizers are applicable to students K–12 but require adaptation for students' cognitive abilities.

Figure 7.3 illustrates a type of information organizer students might use to find differences and commonalities in a set of documents as they begin a study of life in a Japanese-American internment camp. (A digital version of this chart is provided. See pages 205–206.)

Figure 7.3—Historical Data Analysis Guide

Japanese-American Incarceration at Amache Camp Primary Sources	What type of primary source is this?	What was the purpose of the primary source?	When was the primary source produced?	What can we learn from the information in the primary source?
Amache High School student letters				
Photos of the barracks at Amache Camp				
Executive Order 9066				

Chapter 7 Reflection

1. How do you make history and the social studies come alive for students?

2. Consider a unit in which you rely primarily on the use of text-based material. What hands-on strategies or activities might you add to your unit?

3. What activity do you plan to use that will keep students talking for years to come after they leave your classroom? What essential learning do you hope to instill in students through the use of this activity?

Chapter 8

Integrating Social Studies with the Arts

When you think of a people's culture, what comes to mind? Dress? Dance? Food? Traditional music? Pottery or precious artifacts? All of these things are related to the arts. Clearly, when studying a culture, the arts must be part of the exploration.

Recommendations on best practices in social studies call for decreasing the time spent on textbook reading and test taking and increasing the integration of social studies with other areas of the curriculum (Zemelman, Daniels, and Hyde 2012). Social studies concepts are much easier for students to learn the more often they hear related terms, discuss related ideas, and conduct activities across disciplines. This is especially true for the arts, a defining part of history that makes civilizations unique (Levstik and Barton 2015). In addition to exploring the art of a culture, students can create art to express their understanding of social studies concepts. In this chapter, you will find ideas for integrating the arts into social studies lessons by having students dramatize events, view and create art, listen to music, and read powerful literature.

Connecting with Drama

In the social studies, students must learn an enormous amount of information in a given unit of study. According to work summarized by Marzano, Pickering, and Pollock (2012), students need multiple exposures to details to learn them. Providing verbal instruction and visual instruction are helpful, but the effects of dramatizations on learning should not be overlooked. With dramatizations, students can either observe a dramatization or participate in one. Using drama is highly motivating, and students learn to work cooperatively, conduct research, and apply critical thinking and problem-solving skills. It also offers teachers the opportunity to tap into students' multiple intelligences and learning styles—in this case, verbal and kinesthetic learners.

All students, from youngest to oldest, appreciate being able to get up and move at various points during the school day. This allows more blood to pump through their bodies and energize their senses, not to mention it allows blood to flow freely to their brains. This increases their attention spans and helps them think clearly. One way to have students get up and get moving in social studies class is to have them act out concepts. For example, at the primary level, students must understand a variety of geographic terms such as *hill, mountain, river, island,* and *peninsula.* After viewing pictures of these features, students can create hand symbols and motions, gross-motor movements, or rhymes to help them remember each feature's characteristics. Fourth graders studying state geography likely need to know the characteristics of their state's regions. For example, Texas has four regions. A helpful way of teaching the features of each region is to divide the class into four groups and have students dramatize what each region looks like and perform their dramatizations for their classmates. By observing and participating in these dramatizations, students learn the features of the geographic regions, storing them in long-term memory.

Role-Playing

To help students apply and synthesize information they have learned, have students role-play. For this activity, students take on the roles of others and view content from a variety of perspectives. They develop empathy for the people from different periods in time or locations around the world. For example, to help students gain greater understandings for the jobs of craftsmen during the colonial period, you could assign half the class the roles of colonial craftsmen and the other half the roles of customers in the shops. All students choose appropriate colonial names. Sample occupations include the cooper, wig maker, barber, printer, printer's apprentice, wheelwright, blacksmith, and cabinetmaker. Customers include the wives of plantation owners, members of the middle class, members of the gentry, free blacks, slaves, and other craftsmen. Then, provide a wide variety of resources so students can research their roles. Craftsmen would learn about the products and services they provide and the kinds of tools and materials used. They would name their shops and understand why their shops were important in colonial America. Customers would research their needs as well as means of payment for goods and services. Students might also create costumes and props as part of the plan for their role-play situations. Once everything is ready, have students role-play encounters in the shops. To assess the level of students' understanding, interview each shop owner or patron, then rate their level of understanding using a rubric, a rating scale, or a checklist. At the conclusion of the activity, students should discuss and assess the role-play situations. They can express what they learned, how they felt about their roles and the roles of others, and the purpose of doing the activity and its value for increasing understanding of the colonial time period.

Reader's Theater

To engage students in role-playing situations without the need for research, use reader's theater scripts. Reader's theater is a highly motivational strategy for students of all reading levels and abilities. As students take on speaking parts, they convey meaning through intonation, facial expressions, and gestures. Students can also analyze and respond to reader's theater scripts to increase comprehension skills. Through repeated readings, students naturally increase reading fluency as well. All students will need is the script; costumes and props are not necessary.

Living Statues

Another role-playing strategy that might be used as a culminating activity is called Living Statues. Students assume the roles of famous people from a time period under study. Each student creates a living statue to depict the important work from the person's life. Following independent research, students decide upon poses as if they were statues of the people they have selected. Posing one at a time in front of the class, the statues come alive to be interviewed. To make this activity more interactive, half of the class can pose while the second half moves from statue to statue to conduct their own interviews. Then, the students would switch so that the statues become the interviewers and the interviewers become the statues.

Older students may enjoy taking on the role of historical individuals. Instead of students researching all aspects of the individuals' lives (i.e., family, events, major accomplishments), students should focus their research on specific moments in the individuals' lives or on decisions made by them, including the reasons behind the decisions and their lasting impact. Students should look for spoken or written quotes made by their individuals. Then, when they share their information with classmates, they become the individuals in much the same way as re-enactors in Colonial Williamsburg or at other living-history museums.

Connecting with Art

Artwork offers an opportunity for students to both receive information (by studying the artwork of others) and to express information (when students create their own art). This medium is especially valuable in today's social studies classroom. First, artists have been telling history's stories for centuries. The idea of using artwork to help teach students about historical events was first introduced in chapter 5 when using visuals as primary sources. Also, what some might consider being art now (i.e., pottery, wall hangings) was actually once part of a people's culture and daily living. These pieces tell entirely different stories about the past. Students can also use art as a means of self-expression, demonstrating their understanding of particular concepts through a unique format.

Journals and letters provide a human perspective to events in history. However, famous works of art often trigger emotions that words cannot. Think about the emotions portrayed by paintings of American Indians by George Catlin or the monumental landscapes of the romantic era painter, Albert Bierstadt. When students view such pieces, they get a sense of the artist's interpretation of the events and people portrayed in the artwork. By connecting these portrayals with facts and information, students make unique connections with history. These analyses may lead to further questions, generating valuable discussion among students, which, in turn, leads to greater understanding.

Consider the painting *The Jolly Flatboatmen* by George Caleb Bingham. In this picture (Figure 8.1), the characters are carefree, dancing, and playing music on the river. Bingham wanted to paint an energetic, optimistic picture of life in the west. However, students also need to address the question of whether or not this picture is realistic. The painting makes flatboat trips look easy. The men seem relaxed. Students can contrast this portrayal with the real experiences and challenges of transporting cargo on rivers, information they have acquired through text resources. They might also compare the exuberance in the painting with Walt Whitman's description in the poem "I Hear America Singing" from *Leaves of Grass*. After analyzing this topic at length, students can then make comparisons to contemporary life and discuss how cargo is transported today.

Figure 8.1—*The Jolly Flatboatmen* by George Caleb Bingham

Source: National Gallery of Art

Artwork from cultures and individuals can be used in and of themselves as sources of information. When examining Kente cloth from Ghana, pottery from the Hopi people, bronze vessels from China, and stone sculptures from Mexico, students learn about what is (or was) important to a people. They learn about their clothing, food, shelter, architecture, recreation, and technology. They also learn about their religious beliefs and values. High school teachers might choose to include an analysis of artwork from the Byzantine Empire during their study of this era in history. The Metropolitan Museum of Art has a prepared slide show of several artifacts that use stonework, mosaics, ivory, silver, parchment, etc.

Students can analyze these pieces for elements of spiritual symbolism and their appreciation for splendor as well as for Eastern and classical Western influences.

In addition to examining the art of a culture, students can create some form of artwork themselves as a means to express their ideas or to demonstrate their interpretation of facts and events. The creativity required to produce an original piece of art helps students develop critical thinking and problem-solving skills. It also reaches students who learn best through visual means. As with any classroom activity, design the desired outcome so that students demonstrate their understanding of the lesson or unit's learning objectives. Producing art is fun, but be ever mindful of its purpose. Students can create art based on a culture's traditions to better understand how people lived. For instance, when studying the culture of West Africa, students could work on a weaving project to better understand how Kente cloth was created. Or when studying ancient Greece, students can make and decorate a pot to have a better understanding of the craftsmanship displayed by the ancient Greeks.

Another way to integrate art is to ask students to artistically represent a concept that they have learned about. For instance, students can create drawings to represent their knowledge of the five freedoms in the First Amendment. This activity requires students to synthesize their understanding, but in original and artistic formats. In order to successfully complete this assignment, students must consider the five freedoms and why they are important and then create unique ways to symbolically depict this information.

Examining the architecture of a group of people also provides valuable information and insight into a culture. By examining the kinds of materials used in creating the buildings from a particular area or era, students gain geographic understandings, learn about weather conditions, consider population density, and infer mobility issues. They also can discover peoples' values and religious beliefs. And the study of one style of architecture can lead to understanding the interrelatedness and direct influences among civilizations and groups of people. To help guide architectural studies, ask the questions on page 159.

- What is the location and setting of the building?

- For what purpose was it built?

- What are the building materials?

- What kinds of decorations and designs are on the building?

- What words or signs are on the building?

- What is the current use of the building?

- How does design reflect the values of the society?

For example, if a group of students is studying the architecture and structures produced by the ancient Greeks or Romans, its study would include the Parthenon on the Acropolis, the Forum, the Roman Colosseum, and aqueducts. In addition to the questions above, students would research buildings that are currently built in the same styles and consider why those styles are still copied today. Students can gain a newfound appreciation for their hometowns when they see buildings in their local communities that integrate architectural features used in ancient Greece and Rome. Finally, they can consider the question, "What do these buildings tell us about our current values and beliefs?"

The United States government also produces works of art. Students can study the examples for information, and then synthesize their knowledge by creating their own examples. Commemorative stamps and political posters are examples of this type of art. Often, elementary-age children research famous individuals as part of a biography unit. Students can then create their own commemorative stamps depicting the individuals they have studied. They can synthesize their learning by writing letters to the United States Postal Service explaining the significance of the individuals in history and explaining why they feel a stamp should be created

Suggest a new commemorative stamp!
Send suggestions, in writing to:

Citizens' Stamp Advisory Committee
c/o Stamp Development
US Postal Service
475 L'Enfant Plaza SW, Room 3300
Washington, DC 20260-3501

in honor of the person they studied. This abstract activity can easily be turned into a real-life lesson by proposing stamps for consideration to the Citizens' Stamp Advisory Committee, a group that evaluates any and all stamp suggestions that meet the criteria for consideration and makes recommendations for new commemorative stamps.

Public memorials and monuments are designed to honor individuals and the achievements of Americans. Students can create models, drawings, or sketches of their own sculptures and monuments to show how they interpret information. This activity is effective after students have studied a large time period of history. Introduce this idea by showing students examples of various monuments and memorials. Some monuments contain actual sculptures of people, such as Abraham Lincoln in the Lincoln Memorial or Eleanor and Franklin Roosevelt in the FDR Memorial, both in Washington, D.C. Other memorials contain depictions of real people in historical events. An example of this type of monument is the Korean War Memorial in Washington, D.C. Finally, some memorials are more symbolic, such as the Vietnam Veterans Memorial and World War II Memorial in Washington, D.C. and the Statue of Liberty in New York Harbor. As part of the lesson design, students discuss the subject of the honorary memorial, when it was made, and the values it depicts. They then choose what they believe to be the most significant events or individuals that they studied and design their own commemorative sculptures or memorials. You can strengthen the value of this type of activity by having students write a plaque to accompany their memorial, or write a dedication as if it were the first day their memorial was being opened to the public.

Connecting with Music

Auditory learners especially value opportunities to learn through music. Try using the music of a particular time period to help students understand the culture and values of that era. For instance, students may listen to drumming and singing by American Indians or traditional Japanese music using instruments such as the *shakuhachi, koto,* or *shamisen*. Using music in this manner helps students get a flavor for the time period and gain appreciation for the customs of the people.

Students can also listen to music and analyze the lyrics to better understand people's feelings during specific periods of history. For example, studying Vietnam War protest songs of the 1960s can help middle and high school students understand the mindset of United States citizens during that time period. As part of this study, students should recognize the division of beliefs among Americans about the war as well as how domestic events influenced foreign policy of the country. To broaden the learning outcomes within a class, use a modified version of a jigsaw strategy. The only difference is that instead of using text resources, students use song lyrics, perhaps from songs sung by Bob Dylan or Joan Baez. In a jigsaw activity, each group is assigned one song on which to become "experts." Then, students convene in secondary groups so that at least one expert from each of the original groups is present. Each expert shares his or her song with the secondary group. So, although students were responsible for only a small amount of text, they collaborate to determine how their piece fits into the larger picture.

Source: Library of Congress Notated Music Division

The previous examples illustrated how songs might be used with older students. Of course, young students, too, will never pass up opportunities to sing in class! Expand the use of song by working with students to analyze lyrics to patriotic songs such as "The Star Spangled Banner" or "Yankee Doodle Dandy." References to both of these songs, including their histories, can be found at the Library of Congress. Teachers can also use period songs such as "Follow the Drinking Gourd" (a song about the Underground Railroad) to help students reach deeper understanding of historical events. These examples give classroom teachers the chance to connect with their music teachers, expanding students' exposure to social studies topics even further by involving fine arts in content-area learning.

These questions can help students analyze song lyrics. Use students' responses to the questions as an assessment of their learning.

1. List the people, places, and events mentioned in the song.

2. What problems are mentioned in the song? What exact lyrics identify the problem?

3. Are there any repeated phrases? What are they? Why are these words so important that they must be repeated?

4. What is the tone or feeling of the song? What lyrics in the song make you think this?

5. What symbolism was used in the song? List the symbolism and its meaning.

6. Summarize the message or theme of the song.

7. Do you think this song is effective in its intended purpose? Is the message clear? Why or why not?

These questions and ideas were adapted from Fairfax County Public Schools in Virginia.

Connecting with Literature

Chapter 3 explored at length the idea of using a wide variety of reading materials when teaching social studies content. Because of the artistic nature of some literature, it bears mentioning here as well. Picture books, biographies, novels, myths, legends, and even some nonfiction have voice and passion and bring history to life. These books often come in a variety of formats and in a wide range of readability levels, so any student can become engaged with history. Students can read historical narratives to understand the emotions, fears, joys, challenges, and successes of ordinary and extraordinary people. As they read, they may identify with the characters, make connections to their own lives, and activate their curiosity. Through stories, myths, legends, and biographies, students become immersed "in times and cultures of the recent and long-ago past."

When selecting a variety of narratives on a certain topic to use with students, Linda S. Levstik and Keith C. Barton (2015) use the following criteria:

- Is the book good literature and good history?

- Is the story accurate and authentic in details?

- Does it give a flavor of the times with somewhat authentic language?

- Is the historical interpretation sound?

- Are a variety of perspectives included?

- Can students make connections with their own lives?

Informational books can engage students in the lives of people, places, and events throughout history. *Immigrant Kids* and *Children of the Wild West* by Russell Freedman are two examples. The DK Eye Wonder series is another.

Levstik and Barton (2015) suggest the following criteria for choosing nonfiction books:

- What are the qualifications of the author?

- Are the facts accurate and complete?

- Is the book up-to-date and relatively current?

- Does the author distinguish between fact and supposition?

- Does the author provide notes for additional information and sources?

- Is the book well organized? Can it be used for different purposes?

- Are the author's voice and style apparent? Does the author seem to care about the topic?

To illustrate how students can learn from literature, consider a study of the Battle at Gettysburg. Students can use graphic organizers to compare how different authors perceive and record the outcomes of this event. One source of information is the textbook. Another is a nonfiction trade book such as *Eyewitness Reports: The Inquirer's Live Coverage of the American Civil War* by Edward Colimore and *Long Road to Gettysburg* by Jim Murphy. A third source, *Thunder at Gettysburg* by Patricia Lee Gauch, uses poetic form to tell the story of a young girl in Gettysburg. Figure 8.2 shows how students can record information and personal reflections from three different sources. This graphic organizer is easily adaptable for two or four text sources as well. (A digital version of this chart is provided. See page 205.)

Source: Library of Congress Prints and Photographs Division

Figure 8.2—Comparing Perspectives

Textbook	Nonfiction Source	Historical Fiction Source
What facts does the author include?		
What personal experiences does the author include?		
Summarize: What is each text saying?		
Think: What questions do you still have?		
Reflect: What is the value of reading this text?		

Chapter 8 Reflection

1. How could you integrate more drama into a specific unit of study?

2. Consider the literature for a specific unit of study. Identify two fiction books and two nonfiction books that present varying perspectives on the topic. How might you use them in your instruction?

3. What is an example of how you could integrate art and music into a unit that you teach?

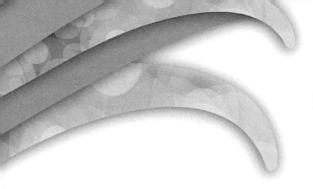

Chapter 9

Assessment

In today's environment and culture of high-stakes testing, pressure to demonstrate success through test scores has given the idea of assessment a rather negative connotation. The unfortunate result in all of this is that the importance of assessment for student learning has been somewhat undermined by this need to provide proof of student learning. The irony is that if assessment for learning is used effectively as a means to inform teachers and students of their progress, then student success on an assessment of learning will naturally follow.

Typically, an assessment of learning is usually summative, while assessment for learning is diagnostic or formative. One single assessment could measure both types of learning if structured for that purpose. Generally, however, an assessment will probably lean more in one direction than the other. (See Figure 9.1.)

Figure 9.1—Assessment of and for Learning

Assessment of Learning	Assessment for Learning
• Evaluates what has been learned to date	• Evaluates learning to decide what to do next
• Informative for those not directly involved in daily learning and teaching	• Formative in nature; designed to assist teachers and students
• Can be presented in a formal report	• Evokes dialogue related to student work
• Summarizes achievement through marks, scores, or grades	• Uses detailed, specific, and descriptive feedback
• Compares the student's learning to either that of other students or the "standard" for a grade level	• Focused on improvement
• Does not need to involve the student	• Involves the student

A complete, well-rounded instructional plan includes both formative and summative assessments. Formative assessments gauge where students are along the learning continuum, from having acquired little to no information to having mastered particular content. This information informs instructional decisions as the unit progresses, perhaps prompting you to review information, include additional activities to support students as they learn new material, or provide extension activities for students who excel with the general content. You will also want to evaluate student learning summatively to assess students' overall performance with regard to the content, perhaps in preparation for assigning grades. The following pages explore both types of assessment within the context of today's social studies classroom.

Assessment Drives Instruction

Teachers should consider assessment in general as ongoing. Any one assessment should directly relate to the lesson and/or unit objectives. Too often, teachers teach content or concepts within a certain time frame, and move on. Time constraints placed on teachers insist they maintain a steady pace as they move through the curriculum. Unfortunately, students who have not mastered the material will not successfully move on. Thus the question becomes, how do teachers know whether their students have mastered the content?

Formative assessments that drive instruction are cyclical in nature. As teachers teach the content objectives, they administer formative assessments along the way. Based on these results, they may make timely adjustments in the learning strategies and activities to better support student learning as they move toward the summative assessment. Rick Stiggins (2007, 62) identifies three key questions related to the process of constructing meaningful formative assessments:

- What are the instructional decisions we hope to make?

- Who is making them?

- What information will be helpful?

Using these questions provides a clear purpose for assessments, and they help both teachers and students stay on track to meet the overall learning targets. The question of how to know that students have mastered the learning objectives should be at the forefront of the lesson design rather than an afterthought. This kind of thinking affects the activities and assignments that are selected for lessons. It also helps teachers hone in on what students need to learn and be able to do. This, in turn, leads to the creation of the deliberate use of learning strategies, instructional activities, and meaningful assessments to meet the objectives.

Ongoing Assessment Strategies for Learning

The previous discussion of assessments could lead one to think that all assessments require a major amount of planning and execution. That is relatively true for summative (of learning) assessments. However, there are a number of quick, easy, effective, and ongoing assessments that can be used to inform teaching.

Exit Cards

To use exit cards, ask students to take a minute to reflect on a question related to the day's lesson, or invite students to simply write explanations of what they learned during class. Each student hands in a card in order to exit the classroom.

For example, say students were studying the concept of manifest destiny. At any point during the unit, you might want to know the extent to which students truly understand its meaning; that, at its core, it was the notion that America's destiny was to expand its borders from sea to sea. You could ask students to draw pictures, sketches, or diagrams, or complete a simple graphic organizer to illustrate the meaning of this broad topic.

After reviewing a set of the exit cards, you can group students by those who understand the content or the concept, and those who show little, if any, understanding. The students who have a strong understanding of the concept may engage in enrichment or extension activities, perhaps an online simulation or further reading. While these students are working independently to extend their learning, you can work with other students to review the material; perhaps having students read excerpts from additional text resources and comparing the information to better understand the concept.

Marzano (2006) suggests that the information on the exit card be presented in a way that is not used to learn the material. In other words, if students read a passage and discuss it, they then should represent what they learned graphically through sketches, diagrams, or drawings. This process involves using an additional part of the brain, thus ensuring that the information has been more thoroughly learned.

Venn Diagrams

One effective use of the Venn diagram is as a means to visually assess student understanding of a concept or an idea. Three circles may be used to compare three related ideas; however, for less complexity, students may begin with two circles to compare two related ideas.

As an example of how to use a Venn diagram to assess students' understanding, consider the political positions of the North and South over the course of the 30 years leading up to the Civil War. You could give each small group or pair of students two different colored circles: one labeled North and the other South. Then, ask students to place their circles in Venn-diagram form to illustrate the similarity of political positions at the following times. The more closely related the two groups' ideas, the more overlap between the circles.

- 1820—Missouri Compromise

- 1850—Fugitive Slave Act and Compromise of 1850

- 1854—Kansas-Nebraska Act

- 1860—Election of Abraham Lincoln

As you give students dates and events, circulate around the classroom and assess the students' circle responses. You can also question students about their positioning of the two circles.

In this example, for the year 1820, the circles should be very nearly on top of one another. With each subsequent date, students should move the circles farther apart until 1860, when there is a relatively small overlap (the South has not yet seceded and still recognizes the validity of the Constitution).

Student-Involved Assessment

Student achievement improves when students are involved in the assessment process, are required to think about their own learning, and articulate what they understand and what they still need to learn (Black and Wiliam 2010). Student involvement in assessment does not mean that students control decisions regarding what will or will not be learned or tested, or that they will assign their own grades. It does mean, however, that students learn to use assessment information to manage their own learning so they understand how they learn best, know exactly where they are in relation to a defined learning target, and plan and take the next steps in their learning. Student-involved classroom assessment works like a mirror that students hold up to watch themselves grow and to feel in control of and to chart their own success. It lets students know and accept that no one is an expert the first time they try something; rather, there is a learning curve that starts low and progresses upward.

Students are involved in the learning process when they do the following:

- use assessment information

- make learning decisions related to their own improvement

- develop an understanding of what quality work looks like

- self assess

- communicate their status and progress toward established learning goals

To become involved in their own assessments and evaluations, students can complete the following:

- Score their work

- Develop evaluation criteria

- Know and apply strategies for improvement

- Reflect on what they know and decide what's next

- Keep records

- Communicate verbally or in writing regarding their progress

- Participate in assessment development

Students can assess their own learning in any number of simple ways. This task helps students track their own progress, and it informs teachers where students are along the learning continuum (from having no knowledge to fully understanding content). Reviewing the results can lead to simple adjustments in the next day's instruction. The ideas that follow illustrate how student self-assessment may be accomplished quickly yet effectively.

3–2–1

With this strategy, students record their thoughts following this outline:

- 3 things I know well

- 2 things that are still a bit unclear

- 1 question I have

Square, Triangle, Circle

With this strategy, students use shapes to record their thoughts about a topic, following these prompts:

- something I am "square" with (I understand fully)

- triangle "points" I want to remember

- something still "circling around" in my mind

Likert Scales

Likert scales have students rate their level of learning on a simple scale (1 to 5, or 1 to 4, for example).

- Using a scale of 1 to 5, students rate their understanding of a concept or content. This can be done just once or at the beginning of the lesson or unit and then again at the end of the lesson or unit. Students can hold their fingers in the air to indicate their personal level of understanding, or to keep the display more private, students can hold their fingers under their chins so that only the teacher sees how students rate themselves.

- Another option is to provide students with physical copies of a scale, such as the one that follows (Figure 9.2). Students can circle their rating for a particular topic (i.e., scarcity) and then write short explanations as to why they rate themselves this way. Students can also ask clarifying questions on their paper, which the teacher may use the next day to start the lesson.

Figure 9.2—Example Likert Scale

1	2	3	4	5
No understanding	Some understanding	Moderate understanding	Good understanding	Complete understanding

Student Response Systems

Many of today's social studies classrooms have student response systems and devices. This electronic program allows the teacher to input questions and answer choices and project them onto a screen for the whole class to see at one time. As each question is posed, students use a response device, sometimes referred to as a "clicker," to choose their answer. Or some response systems allow students to "text" short responses into the program. Their data is stored, and the teacher may pull up a report with each student's score (as well as open-ended responses, if there are any). This particular assessment strategy provides instant feedback for both students and teachers. After the class responds, students can see how many students selected each answer choice, and then the correct answer is revealed. This allows teachers to have discussions as needed based on the students' responses. If all or most students answer one question correctly, the teacher can say "Good job" and move on. If a majority of students miss any one particular question, the teacher may stop and discuss the question and answer choices, clarifying concepts and ideas on an as-needed basis. When the results are regularly displayed and graphed, students become motivated to improve their score from the previous session.

Student response systems are perfect for quick formative assessments. In this case, the teacher may pose just three questions to the class. Students may also enter responses for formal (summative) quizzes and tests. The teacher saves time grading papers, and students know instantly how they performed on the test. The teacher may opt to conduct the multiple choice portion of a longer summative assessment using the student response system then have students respond using paper-pencil (or electronic word processing) to answer constructed response questions. Regardless of the extent to which they are used, student response systems are a valuable part of assessment in today's social studies classroom.

Models for Constructing Assessments

The information found in Figure 9.3 serves as a means for thinking about a lesson from the perspective of an assessor. Consider the following questions and how they would be answered using the information provided in Figure 9.3.

- What is the purpose of my lesson or activity? (Mastery of content? Reasoning? Skills? A combination?)

- How will I most effectively measure the learning of my students, the degree to which they have met my goals? (Selected response? Products? Performance assessment? Personal communication? A combination?) How will I communicate their progress to my students? To their parents?

- What learning activities will I develop to help students use the content to practice the skills or reasoning that I will be assessing?

Responses to these questions enable you to begin to think about the strategies and tools you will use to measure student progress. Remember, the type of assessment you use to gather data about student learning needs to be compatible with the purpose of the assessment. In other words, selected response items such as true and false or multiple choice will not yield much, if any, information about students' abilities to develop a historical thesis based on a set of documents. Thus, if the purpose of a lesson is to teach students to analyze documents so that they may answer a historical question prompted by the material contained in primary source documents, an assessment yielding such results is more in order than a multiple choice test. The information in Figure 9.3 demonstrates the connection between the overall learning targets and various types of assessments.

Figure 9.3—Learning Targets and Assessment Methods

	Mastery of Content (Knowledge)	Reasoning	Skills
Selected Response (multiple choice, true-false, etc.)	Can be used to assess content knowledge—as can all five formats	Can be an excellent way to access some key kinds of reasoning—but not all kinds	Can only test for mastery of prerequisite procedural knowledge
Constructed Response (short answer, time line, visual representation, etc.)	Can be used to assess student ability to reconstruct knowledge and apply it to a new situation	Can be used to assess some kinds of reasoning related to student ability to use knowledge	Can be used to analyze student use of knowledge to construct new understanding
Products (essay, portfolio, model, etc.)	Can serve to assess student mastery of complex structures of knowledge	Can provide a window into reasoning	Can ask students to describe the complex "how to" procedural knowledge
Performance Assessment (oral presentation, simulation, debate, etc.)	Unless carefully constructed with a solid rubric, may not be as effective as the other three methods	Can watch student in the process of problem solving and draw inferences regarding proficiency	Can observe and evaluate skills as demonstrated
Personal Communication (oral questioning, observations, interview, etc.)	Can assess small domains of knowledge when short-term record keeping is required	Can ask student to "think out loud" to examine problem solving proficiency	Can be a strong match when the skill is oral communication proficiency; can ask student to describe and discuss complex "how to" procedural knowledge

Figure 9.4 lists the various activities that can be used as the basis for different types of assessment. Alignment of the assessment to the learning target is critical. Additionally, performance-based assessments require a strong rubric that clearly delineates what is being assessed.

Figure 9.4—Options to Assess Student Learning

Selected Response Items	Performance-Based Assessments		
	Constructed Response	Products	Performances
Multiple choice True-false Matching **Fill in the blank** • words • phrases	**Short Answer** • sentence(s) • paragraph(s) • label a diagram "Show your work." • time line **Visual Representation** • concept web or map • graph/chart • matrix • illustration • flow chart • Venn diagram or other graphic organizer	**Factual** • paragraph or essay • research paper • video or audio summary • slide show presentation • spreadsheet • news article or editorial **Creative** • letter • poem • portfolio • art exhibit • model • song	**Independent** • oral presentation or monologue • demonstration • simulation • dramatic reading • enactment **Collaborative** • debate • skit/play • interview

Adapted from Jay McTighe 2011.

Checklists and Rubrics

The idea of using checklists and rubrics was first introduced in chapter 6 as an essential and integral part of assigning research projects and reports. However, rubrics and performance task assessment lists, previously referred to as rating scales, serve many more purposes than just evaluating research projects. Students involved in performance-based assessment of any kind deserve to know how their efforts will be evaluated. For this reason, a summary of how to use checklists and rubrics is included in this chapter as well.

A performance-task assessment list (rating scale) provides an alternative to a rubric. It is a set of criteria that has assigned point values. Checklists enable you to clearly identify the criteria you value as part of the project's completion. This may be quality components, such as the use of grammatical conventions, the content of the project, or how well it is organized. Consider weighing lesser-important details with fewer points so that students are more focused on the quality and correctness of their work rather than the color of ink they use. Sharing such a checklist with students along with the assignment is valuable so that they understand how their work will be evaluated before they begin.

Questions to consider when creating a performance-task assessment list include the following:

- What is the content knowledge needed to demonstrate mastery?

- What are the process skills students need to be successful?

- What are the components of the performance task?

- How many points will be allocated to each component?

To realize the performance-task assessment list's greatest potential, provide students with models of student work that illustrate the full continuum of quality (exemplary, acceptable, and not acceptable). One benefit of a performance-task assessment list is that it allows you to prioritize expectations based on the components listed or by adjusting the number of points assigned to each component.

A rubric is an objective set of criteria expressed as a scale and used to assess levels of student performance in comparison to clearly articulated standards. It is distinguishable from other forms of criteria in that a narrative describing the components that meet each level of performance accompanies each level on a rubric. Rubrics can be either holistic or analytic:

- Holistic rubrics give one rating for the work. They are useful for summative assessments where the student will not be given the opportunity to learn from the feedback.

- Analytic rubrics give individual ratings for components of the work. They are more useful to students in identifying areas for improvement.

Rubrics can be generic or task specific. Models of student work to accompany evaluation rubrics help students have clear pictures of both the criteria for how their efforts will be evaluated and what this looks like on paper. Ideally, students would see a range of products that meet various levels of the evaluation criteria. These not only provide models for students to emulate, but they also clarify distinctions among the levels of performance.

With advancements in technology, designing and creating rubrics is much less time consuming than in years past. There are online rubric making programs, some of which are free while others require paid accounts. Another electronic option is to create a template using a spreadsheet program. Once the template is complete, you need only modify it slightly to match the evaluation criteria for each assessment. Or you can embed a table into a word processing document to formulate your rubric or performance task list/rating scale. The advantages of using word processing are that you can add titles, headings, images or clip art, signature lines, etc. Some of these options are not offered in spreadsheet software.

The following guidelines will help you design and use rubrics for any assessment purpose, regardless of the format or style.

• Begin with a description of the criteria that applies to the proficient student. Once that level has been defined, describing the performance of other levels becomes less difficult.

• Avoid counting criteria when possible. Often, when numbers are used to differentiate between performance levels, the quality of the response or example tends to suffer. Consider the dilemma of five mediocre examples versus three excellent examples. Has the student achieved the advanced level because of a greater number of criteria?

• Use anchor papers or models of student work representing each level of performance to help students better understand exactly what is expected.

• Conduct a scoring workshop in which students are given the rubric and the anchor papers and asked to score each one and assign it a proficiency level. This gets students looking critically at the rubric and understanding the differentiation among the levels.

- Involve students in the creation of the rubric. Share the struggle to articulate criteria that clearly indicate levels of quality.

- Encourage students to assess their own performances using the rubric.

- Develop a reflection guideline that prompts students to begin thinking about their achievements and how they might be improved.

The rubrics that follow (Figures 9.5–9.7; Digital versions of these rubrics are provided. See pages 205–206.) demonstrate several examples of rubrics teachers might use to evaluate student learning. Figure 9.5 shows a four-point rubric with levels defined as unsatisfactory, partially proficient, proficient, and advanced. A fifth point ("0") can be used to indicate that the student did not take the assessment or that this element was omitted.

Figure 9.5—Historical Advertisement Rubric

	No indication of work	Unsatisfactory	Partially Proficient	Proficient	Advanced
	0	1	2	3	4
Content of advertisement demonstrates student's understanding of historical concepts.					
Advertisement shows connection to historical context.					
Advertisement contains necessary information or facts.					
Concept is original, persuasive, and appealing to the audience.					
Information is well presented: effective, concise, and error-free.					
Artwork is creative, colorful, and neat.					

Adapted from Fairfax Country Public Schools in Virginia

Sometimes, the learning aspects can be conflated with production aspects when constructing rubrics. Notice how the first two items in the list of criteria in the rubric in Figure 9.5 address student learning, but the third through sixth items address the product students are to make. In this instance, the teacher appears to value the construct of the product over the content. For example, if a student satisfactorily completed all the tasks and produced an advertisement that was persuasive and appealing in an effective, concise, and error-free manner with colorful, creative, and neat artwork (3 points × 4 criteria) but demonstrated little understanding of the historical concepts and context (1 point × 2 criteria), he or she could achieve an overall score of 2.3 (partially proficient) when, in fact, the student only demonstrated proficiency in creativity.

Compare the previous rubric to the one in Figure 9.6.

Figure 9.6—Rubric for Information Processing

4	Analyzes information in detail, accurately and insightfully determining whether it is credible and relevant to a specific task
3	Accurately determines whether information is credible and relevant to a specific task
2	Makes some significant errors in determining whether information is credible and relevant to a specific task
1	Makes little or no attempt to determine whether information is credible and relevant to a specific task, or totally misjudges the relevance and credibility of information
0	No indication of work

Source: Chappuis et al. 2013

This particular rubric might be useful when evaluating students' theses, perhaps from a document-based questioning assignment (see chapter 5). The criteria in this rubric identifies the standard being measured, assess the value of information, and articulate the gradations of student performance. They also allow you to assess and communicate, in a fairly concrete manner, the abilities of students to process the information they have been given and to synthesize it into a formal position paper.

Unique, original rubrics are not necessary for each assignment. Just as the previous rubric was applied to a specific assignment, a generic rubric, such as the one in Figure 9.7, can be used for a variety of assignments as long as both the teachers and their students understand what each descriptor means. Again, anchor papers that clearly delineate the differences between levels are essential for successful use of a rubric like the one in Figure 9.7.

Figure 9.7—Generic Information Rubric

	Rubric for Information		Rubric for Information for Younger Students
4	The student has a complete and detailed understanding of the information important to the topic.	4	The student completely understands the important information. The student knows details about the information.
3	The student has a complete understanding of the information important to the topic.	3	The student understands the important information.
2	The student has an incomplete understanding of the topic or misconceptions about some of the information.	2	The student does not completely understand the important information, or the student's thinking shows some mistakes about the information.
1	The student's understanding of the topic is incomplete, or the student has so many misconceptions that he or she cannot be said to understand the topic.	1	The student does not understand the important information. The student's thinking shows considerable mistakes about the information.
0	There is not enough information to make a judgment.	0	The student does not try to do the task.

Source: Marzano 2006

These rubric examples demonstrate the difference between ones that measure what students have learned and ones that measure what students have produced. When informing parents of their children's mastery of content, teachers should choose or create rubrics to accurately evaluate what they wish to measure: student learning or student products.

Chapter 9 Reflection

1. Think about assessment for (and of) learning. Identify assessments you have given that are examples of each.

2. Consider the assessments you just identified. What instructional objectives are they designed to measure? Which achievement targets do they meet (mastery of content, reasoning, or skills)? Do the assessments match the learning objectives and achievement targets?

3. If not, what might you change about them?

4. Use what you learned about rubric development by reading this chapter. Assess a rubric you currently use. What might you change?

Chapter 10

Putting It All Together

This book concludes by sharing examples of lessons that integrate different disciplines and apply some of the strategies and content outlined in this book. The following two examples illustrate the concept of "working smart." Through these methods of integrating instruction, students will have the opportunity to apply skills and thinking processes in an active, thoughtful, interdisciplinary manner.

Mini-Unit: Harriet Tubman and the Underground Railroad

This mini-unit on Harriet Tubman and the Underground Railroad integrates reading skills with the examination of art, primary sources, online interactive activities, and music. Knowing the time constraints faced in all classrooms, the question becomes, "How can I integrate as much as possible and still help students reach the essential objectives?" The lesson-planning guide introduced in chapter 1 (pages 23–25) becomes a helpful tool in orchestrating activities that engage students while teaching key concepts and developing important skills.

Source: New York Public Library Digital Collections

As noted on the guide, the first step is to identify the standards, learning targets, and questions that will focus student learning. For this mini-unit, these are:

- **Standard:** Generate questions about individuals and groups who have shaped significant historical changes and continuities.

- **Learning Targets:** I can explain what the Underground Railroad was and why it was important. I can explain Harriet Tubman's role in the Underground Railroad.

- **Compelling Question:** Why would people risk traveling on the Underground Railroad?

- **Supporting Questions:** What was the Underground Railroad? What people were involved? What was the route? Why was it important?

Next, consider how to assess and build students' background knowledge. To introduce this unit to fifth graders, I have chosen to read aloud *Moses: When Harriet Tubman Led Her People to Freedom* by Carole Boston Weatherford. The book introduces Harriet Tubman, gives background on slavery, and sets the stage for an exploration of the Underground Railroad.

After the read-aloud, students rotate through learning centers stocked with materials that they observe, analyze, and interpret using directed reading and thinking questions that accompany the resources. Working in small groups, students will collaborate to build their knowledge about Harriet Tubman and the Underground Railroad. Students spend about one class period at each center, with an extra day at the end of the unit for them to finish up incomplete tasks or revisit a center at which they want to spend more time. Following is a brief description of the materials and tasks at each of the five centers.

Center 1: Harriet Tubman

This center features photographs of Harriet Tubman, such as the one shown in Figure 10.1, along with biographies and articles about her at various reading levels. Students work in pairs to write eulogies for Harriet Tubman, highlighting her accomplishments as a leader of the Underground Railroad.

Figure 10.1—Harriet Tubman

Source: The Library of Congress Prints and Photographs Division

Center 2: Underground Railroad

This center contains maps of the Underground Railroad, including one from the time period as shown in Figure 10.2. It also contains re-creations of primary sources as well as firsthand accounts of people who traveled on and supported the Underground Railroad such as Levi Coffin's account of his station in Newport, Indiana. (You can access this and other historical documents at PBS's Africans in America website.) Students take notes on the documents, and then write summary statements about the Underground Railroad.

Figure 10.2—"The Underground Railroad" by Charles T. Webber

Source: The Library of Congress Prints and Photographs Division

Center 3: Using Primary Sources

Place a primary source or re-creation of a primary document from the time period in this center such as the Broadside shown in Figure 10.3. Students work together to figure out what the purpose of the document was, who might have written it, and what other details they can learn about the time from the document.

Figure 10.3—1847 Broadside

$200 Reward

RANAWAY from the subscriber, on the night of Thursday, the 20th of September.

Five Negro Slaves,

To-wit, one Negro man, his wife, and three children.

The man is a black negro, full height, very erect, his face a little thin. He is about forty years of age, and calls himself Washington Reed, and is known by the name of Washington. He is probably well dressed, possibly takes with him an ivory headed cane, and is of good address. Several of his teeth are gone.

A reward of $150 will be paid for their apprehension, so that I can get them, if taken within one hundred miles of St. Louis, and $200 if taken beyond that.

WM Russell

ST. Louis, Oct. 1, 1847

Source: Library of Congress Rare Book and Special Collections Division, African American Odyssey

Center 4: Music of the Time

This center contains music and lyrics to spirituals such as "Go Down Moses" and "Follow the Drinking Gourd." After students listen to the music and read through the lyrics, they talk together about why such songs were written and how they helped slaves.

Center 5: Computer Explorations

Students explore two interactive sites about slavery and the Underground Railroad: National Geographic's Underground Railroad: Journey to Freedom interactive activity (http://www.nationalgeographic.org/media/underground-railroad-journey-freedom/), and PBS's Slave Memories site (www.pbs.org/wnet/slavery/memories/index_flash.html).

As students rotate through the centers, they also complete a data retrieval chart (Figure 10.4) listing information they learn from each center. (A digital version of this chart is provided. See pages 205–206.)

Figure 10.4—Data Retrieval Chart

Center Number:	Name
Sources (describe)	
Facts and Information	
Inferences	
Questions I Have	

When students have completed their rotation through the centers, they come together as a whole class for a concluding discussion that focuses on the purpose of the Underground Railroad, key individuals involved, feelings of slaves and slave owners, and student reactions. Students can also discuss the points of view of the creator or writer of the different items at each center. Students compare and contrast information, share inferences made about each item, and evaluate the usefulness of each item in learning about the importance of the Underground Railroad.

In terms of assessment, the brief writing activities students complete at the centers and the data retrieval charts can serve as informal assessments, and students' contribution to both small-group and whole-class discussions can be assessed as well. For a more formal assessment, students could write interview questions for Tubman and then write responses they think she would provide based on facts and inferences they made from the center activities.

Using Water to Teach Civics, Economics, Geography, and History

The previous mini-unit demonstrated the integration of art, music, history, primary sources, literature, texts, and writing. The overview of the study that follows integrates the four social studies disciplines—civics, economics, geography, and history (as indicated by the 11 standards listed below)—through the study of water. In this unit, the expectation is that teaching a global concept to students via the four disciplines will then enable them to apply those concepts to other content areas. The learning objectives for this unit are as follows:

- Understands and knows how to analyze chronological relationships and patterns

- Understands that scarcity of productive resources requires choices that generate opportunity costs

- Understands characteristics of different economic systems, economic institutions, and economic incentives

- Understands the concept of prices and the interaction of supply and demand in a market economy

- Understands the roles government plays in the United States economy

- Understands patterns of human settlement and their causes

- Understands the changes that occur in the meaning, use, distribution, and importance of resources

- Understands how geography is used to interpret the past

- Understands global development and environmental issues

- Understands ideas about civic life, politics, and government

- Understands the sources, purposes, and functions of law and the importance of the rule of law for the protection of individual rights and the common good

The historical part of the study begins with a time line activity that asks students to think about human development around a western river from the sixteenth century through the twenty-first century. Students, divided into collaborative work groups, read brief histories of the land and the river at different points in time. Each group is asked to portray that information graphically on a pre-prepared piece of chart paper that contains a portion of a river. When groups combine their pieces of chart paper, they form a river time line that traces its development over the course of five centuries.

The majority of the study focuses on economic concepts. Students experience a series of lessons and activities designed to teach them economic concepts that are key to understanding the issue of water. Included in those concepts are scarcity, opportunity costs and benefits, property rights, supply and demand, choice, incentives, Tragedy of the Commons, and the Diamond Water Paradox. Students learn these concepts in a variety of active, hands-on lessons by gathering data of their own water use, considering its uses and ways to ameliorate their thinking about how they value and use water. The role-play scenarios put them in the positions of various members of a community who use water for very different reasons. They take a step back in history to consider the importance of water to *Romeo and Juliet* as compared to diamonds and contemplate the reasons that diamonds are more valued than water. Students then explore the concept of property rights and how they apply to the use and ownership of water in various geographic areas of the United States. Finally, they look at the concept of diminishing marginal returns to determine at which point the cleaning of water is no longer economically advantageous.

After students have learned about the economic aspects of water, they undertake a study of water from a political perspective investigating related public policy and legal issues. They study the structure and function of government to better understand the groups involved in water issues and various organizations, both private and public, that are interested in water policy. Students then engage in a WebQuest to continue their study. Each student, or group of students, is given an identity that reflects one of the stakeholder's interests in water. Students research water issues from their stakeholders' perspectives and prepare presentations before a legislative hearing committee to present solutions to the water issue and defend their points of view. The WebQuest is also designed to allow students to practice the assessment for the unit in groups.

When the WebQuest presentations end, students are given the performance assessment that assigns them the role of president and CEO of a research company whose clients are interest groups throughout the state. Each student is to produce an action plan for his or her clients who wish to change public policy or solve a problem related to a particular issue. Students choose their own issues and apply the understanding of historical, geographic, economic, and political concepts they have learned. Specifically, students are asked to produce a time line that ties their issues to its nineteenth century antecedents and an overview that identifies a problem or an issue existing in the state, discuss its background, and identify and describe the public policy in existence that relates to the issue. Students are asked to prepare proposals for making changes to the existing public policy or suggest several solutions to the problem. In that proposal, students are to discuss the economic concepts that apply to their solutions and identify and defend the solutions they believe best address the issues. Finally, students provide lists of agencies and organizations related to their issues, identify the levels (local, state, federal) of involvement, and explain how the interests of the agency or organization support their solutions.

A rubric that measures student understanding of each component of the assessment evaluates the students' success in the project. The proficient student product is defined in Figure 10.5.

Figure 10.5—Proficient Student Attributes

Time line	• Time line illustrates all conventions (chronological order, spatial and scale considerations) • Time line events are relevant to issue • Includes events related to the issue from the nineteenth century to today
Overview	• Explanation identifies a particular problem or aspect of the issue as it exists in the state today • Relevant nineteenth century antecedents of the issue are identified • Public policy is related to the identified issue • Relationship between public policy and issue is accurately described
Proposal	• Proposal offers two or more alternative solutions to change the policy that are relevant to the chosen issues • Each solution identifies a relevant economic concept • Each solution discusses the relationship between identified economic concepts and the issue
Recommendation	• One solution is identified as "best" • Explanation contains the reasons why the choice was made • Recommendation indicates a plan of action to be taken that reflects the concept of citizen involvement in public affairs
Agencies	• A list of agencies and organizations related to the issues is included • Level (federal, state, local) of government or scope of organization is identified for most agencies or organizations • Explanation of each agency and how it relates to the issue is accurate in most cases

Final Thoughts

Today's social studies classroom is exciting, relevant, and hands on. As time constraints for teaching the social studies have become tighter and tighter, educators must find ways to teach the concepts and content in manners that address and incorporate varieties of disciplines. Social studies content offers many opportunities for students to read, write, and apply critical-thinking skills. Through integrated learning opportunities, students can learn social studies content and apply learning from across disciplines in meaningful, relevant, and engaging activities, which they will remember for many years long after class has ended.

Chapter 10 Reflection

1. Consider a social studies unit that you currently teach. What examples of music, art, literature, and primary sources could you use in this unit?

2. What social studies lessons or units do you currently teach that can be best adapted to include the content and skills of other disciplines? How do you think you might accomplish this?

3. Map out a plan to integrate other disciplines during a favorite social studies unit. Also include an assessment plan and rubric.

Appendix A

References Cited

Allen, Janet. 2014. *Tools for Teaching Academic Vocabulary*. Portland: Stenhouse.

Allen, Janet, and Christine Landaker. 2005. *Reading History: A Practical Guide to Improving Literacy*. New York: Oxford University Press.

Bain, Robert. 2007. "Organization of American Historians, Teaching American History Grant Session." March 19.

Beck, Isabel L., M. McKeown, and L. Kucan. 2013. *Bringing Words to Life, Second Edition*. New York: Guilford Press.

Beer, Kylene. 2003. *When Kids Can't Read What Teachers Can Do: A Guide for Teachers 6–12*. Portsmouth: Heinemann.

Black, Paul, and Dylan Wiliam. 2010. "Inside the Black Box: Raising Standards Through Classroom Assessment." *Phi Delta Kappan* 92 (1).

Buehl, Doug. 2013. *Classroom Strategies for Interactive Learning, 4th Edition*. Newark: International Reading Association.

Center for Civic Education. "Project Citizen." www.civiced.org/programs/project-citizen.

Chappuis, Jan, Rick J. Stiggins, Steve Chappuis, and Judith Arter. 2013. *Classroom Assessment for Student Learning: Pearson New International Edition: Doing it Right—Using it Well*. Harlow: Pearson Education.

Conklin, Wendy. 2015. *Analyzing and Writing with Primary Sources*. Huntington Beach: Shell Education.

Constitutional Rights Foundation. "Active Citizenship Today (ACT) Field Guide." www.crf-usa.org/.

Duke, Nell K., and P. David Pearson. 2008. "Effective Practices for Developing Reading Comprehension." *Journal of Education* 189 (1/2): 107.

Duplass, James A. 2011. *Teaching Elementary Social Studies: Strategies, Standards, and Internet Resources, Third Edition*. Belmont: Wadsworth Cengage Learning.

Fountas, Irene C. and Gay Su Pinnell. 2010. "What Is the Guided Reading Teaching Method?" www.fpblog.heinemann.com/post/2010/08/02/what-is-guided-reading-teaching.aspx.

Frayer, Dorothy, Wayne C. Frederick, and Herbert J. Klausmeier. 1969. *A Schema for Testing the Level of Concept Mastery. Working Paper No. 16*. Madison: Wisconsin Research and Development Center for Cognitive Learning.

Gardner, Howard. 2011. *Frames of Mind: The Theory of Multiple Intelligences Third Edition*. New York: Basic Books.

Hackett, Mollie. 2013. "The DBQ and Close Reading." *The DBQ Project*. dbqproject.com/wp/?p=39.

Harvard Business Publishing. 2015. "Teaching with Simulations." hbsp.harvard.edu/list/simulations-feature.

Harvey, Stephanie, and Anne Goudvis. 2007. *Strategies That Work: Teaching Comprehension for Understanding and Engagement, Second Edition*. Portland, ME: Stenhouse Publishers.

Holt, JoBea. 2012. *Using Google Earth: Bring the World into Your Classroom, Grades 6–8*. Huntington Beach: Shell Education.

International Society of Technology Education. "ISTE Standards." www.iste.org/standards/standards/iste-standards.

Jones, Raymond. "Word Map." www.readingquest.org/pdf/wordmap.pdf.

Keene, Jennifer. 2006. *Unpacking the Historical Thinking Behind the United States and the First World War*. Kansas City: Gilder Lehrman Institute.

Kopp, Kathleen. 2008. *Learning Through Writing: Authentic Writing Activities for the Content Areas*. Gainesville: Maupin House Publishing.

———. 2013. *Strategies for Writing in the Social Studies Classroom*. Gainesville: Maupin House Publishers.

Lemov, Doug, Colleen Driggs, and Erica Woolway. 2016. *Reading Reconsidered: A Practical Guide to Rigorous Literacy Instruction*. San Francisco: Jossey-Bass.

Levstik, Linda S., and Keith C. Barton. 2015. *Doing History: Investigating with Children in Elementary and Middle Schools, 5th Edition*. Mahwah: Lawrence Erlbaum Associates, Publishers.

Library of Congress. n.d. *Using Primary Sources*. www.loc.gov/teachers/usingprimarysources/.

Lipton, Laura, and Deborah Hubble. 2009. *More Than 100 Ways to Student-Centered Literacy, Second Edition*. Thousand Oaks: Corwin Press.

Macceca, Stephanie. 2007. *Reading Strategies for Social Studies*. Huntington Beach: Shell Education.

Marzano, Robert J. 2006. *Classroom Assessment and Grading that Work*. Alexandria: Association for Supervision and Curriculum Development.

Marzano, Robert J., Debra J. Pickering, and Jane E. Pollock. 2012. *Classroom Instruction That Works: Research-Based Strategies for Increasing Student Achievement, 2nd Edition*. Alexandria: Association for Supervision and Curriculum Development.

McREL. 2015. "Standards." www2.mcrel.org/compendium/.

McTighe, Jay. 2011. *Developing and Using Rubrics to Evaluate and Improve Student Performance*. jaymctighe.com/wordpress/wp-content/uploads/2013/04/Webinar-Rubrics-9.27.131.pdf.

Moore, David W., Sharon A. Moore, Patricia M. Cunningham, and James W. Cunningham. 2010. *Developing Readers and Writers in the Content Areas K–12, 6th Edition*. Boston: Allyn & Bacon.

Moss, Connie M., Susan M. Brookhart, and Beverly A. Long. 2011. "Knowing Your Learning Target." *Educational Leadership* 68: 6. www.ascd.org/publications/educational-leadership/mar11/vol68/num06/Knowing-Your-Learning-Target.aspx.

National Archives and Records Administration. "Document Analysis Worksheet." www.archives.gov/education/lessons/worksheets/document.html.

National Council for the Social Studies. 2010. *National Curriculum Standards for Social Studies: A Framework for Teaching, Learning, and Assessment.* Silver Spring, MD.

———. 2013. *The College, Career, and Civic Life (C3) Framework for Social Studies State Standards: Guidance for Enhancing the Rigor of K–12 Civics, Economics, Geography, and History.* Silver Spring, MD.

———. "A State Led Effort to Develop Standards in Social Studies." Last modified March 31, 2011. www.socialstudies.org/statecreatedstandards.

National Governors Association Center for Best Practices, Council of Chief State School Officers. 2010. "Common Core Standards." Washington, DC: National Governors Association Center for Best Practices, Council of Chief State School Officers. www.corestandards.org.

Ogle, Donna, Ronald M. Klemp, and Bill McBride. 2007. *Building Literacy in Social Studies: Strategies for Improving Comprehension and Critical Thinking.* Alexandria: Association for Supervision and Curriculum Development.

Schwartz and Raphael. 2012. "Concept of Definition Map." Adapted by Raymond Jones. www.readingquest.org/strat/cdmap.html.

Smilkstein, Rita. 2011. *We're Born to Learn: Using the Brain's Natural Learning Process to Create Today's Curriculum 2nd Edition.* Thousand Oaks: Corwin Press.

Stanford History Education Group. "Evaluating Information: The Cornerstone of Civic Online Reasoning." sheg.stanford.edu/upload/V3LessonPlans/Executive%20Summary%2011.21.16.pdf. November 22, 2016.

Stiggins, Rick. 2007. *Ahead of the Curve: The Power of Assessment to Transform Teaching and Learning.* Edited by Douglas Reeves. Bloomington: Solution Tree.

Sundem, Garth, and Kristi Pikiewicz. 2005. *American History Activities.* Huntington Beach: Shell Education.

Townsend, Robert B. 2013. *History's Babel: Scholarship, Professionalization, and the Historical Enterprise in the United States, 1880–1940.* Chicago: University of Chicago Press.

University of California, Berkeley. 2012. "Evaluating Web Pages: Techniques to Apply and Questions to Ask." www.lib.berkeley.edu/TeachingLib/Guides/Internet/Evaluate.html.

Vacca, Richard, and Jo Anne Vacca. 2016. *Content Area Reading: Literacy and Learning Across the Curriculum, Enhanced Pearson eText with Loose-Leaf Version—Access Card Package, 12th Edition.* New York: Addison-Wesley Educational Publishers, Inc.

Wessels, Stephanie. 2012. *The Importance of Activating and Building Knowledge.* Lincoln: University of Nebraska—Lincoln.

"What are the Humanities?" *Ohio Humanities Council.* Last modified 2015. www.ohiohumanities.org/about/.

Wineburg, Sam. 2016. "Why Historical Thinking is Not About History." *AASLH History News* (Spring): 13–16.

Wormeli, Rick. 2005. *Summarization in Any Subject.* Alexandria: Association for Supervision and Curriculum Development.

Zemelman, Steven, Harvey Daniels, and Arthur Hyde. 2012. *Best Practice: New Standards for Teaching and Learning in America's Schools.* Portsmouth: Heinemann.

Appendix B

Additional Resources

Cohan, George, M. n.d. "Yankee Doodle Dandy."

Colimore, Edward. 2004. *Eyewitness Reports: The Inquirer's Live Coverage of the American Civil War*. Philadelphia: Philadelphia Newspapers, Inc.

Davidson, James West, and Mark Hamilton Lytle. 2009. *After the Fact: The Art of Historical Detection. Sixth Edition*. New York: McGraw-Hill Education.

DK Eye Wonder series. 2002. New York: DK Publishing.

Eubank, Patricia Reeder. 2002. *Seaman's Journal: On the Trail with Lewis and Clark*. Nashville: Ideals Children's Books.

Forbes, Esther. 2011. Johnny Tremain. New York: HMH Books for Young Readers.

Freedman, Russell. 1995. *Immigrant Kids*. New York: Puffin Books.

———. 1983. *Children of the Wild West*. New York: Clarion Books.

Gauch, Patricia Lee. *Thunder at Gettysburg*. 2003. Honesdale: Calkins Creek.

Gerwin, David, and Jack Zevin. 2003. *Teaching U.S. History as Mystery*. Portsmouth: Heinemann.

Grossman, Patricia, and Enrique O. Sanchez. 1994. *Saturday Market*. New York: Lothrop, Lee & Shepard Books.

Jurmain, Suzanne Tripp. 2006. *George Did It*. New York: Puffin Books.

Key, Francis Scott. 1814. "The Star Spangled Banner." Baltimore, MD.

Kopp, Kathleen. 2013. *Strategies for Writing in the Social Studies Classroom*. Gainesville: Maupin House.

Lawrence, Jacob. 1995. *The Great Migration: An American Story.* New York. HarperCollins Children's Books.

McCunn, Ruthanne Lum. 1998. *Pie-Biter.* New York: Shen's Books.

Murphy, Jim. 1992. *Long Road to Gettysburg.* New York: Clarion Books.

Rabin, Staton. 1994. *Casey Over There.* New York: Harcourt Children's Books.

Raven, Margo Theis. 2002. *Mercedes and the Chocolate Pilot.* Chelsea, MI: Sleeping Bear Press.

Roberts, Randy J., and James S. Olson. 2007. *American Experiences.* 2 vols. New York: Pearson Education.

Seuss, Dr. 1984. *The Butter Battle Book.* New York: Random House.

Sommer, Barbara W., and Mary Kay Quinlan. 2009. *The Oral History Manual.* Lanham: Alta Mira Press.

Weatherford, Carole Boston. 2006. *Moses: When Harriet Tubman Led Her People to Freedom.* New York: Hyperion Books.

Winters, Jeanette. 1992. *Follow the Drinking Gourd.* New York: Dragonfly Books.

Appendix C

Online Resources

America's Story	http://www.americaslibrary.gov
Classroom Zoom, Simulation: Feudal Candy	http://www.classroomzoom.com/lessons/386/simulation-feudal-candy
Colonial Williamsburg	http://www.history.org
Discovery Education	http://www.discoveryeducation.com/
Discovery Education "We the People: A History"	http://www.discoveryeducation.com/teachers/free-lesson-plans/we-the-people-a-history.cfm
EBSCO	http://www.ebscohost.com/
Fact Monster	http://www.factmonster.com/
Google Earth™	http://earth.google.com
Google Maps™	http://maps.google.com
History Guide, The Journal of Christopher Columbus (1492)	http://www.historyguide.org/earlymod/columbus.html
The Invention Factory: Thomas Edison's Laboratories	http://www.nps.gov/nr/twhp/wwwlps/lessons/25edison/25edison.htm
The Jamestown Online Adventure from History Globe	http://www.historyglobe.com/jamestown/jamestowngame.htm
Kids and History "1607 Journey to Jamestown"	http://kidsandhistory.net/1607/thebeginning.html
Lewis and Clark and the Revealing of America	http://www.loc.gov/exhibits/lewisandclark/
Library of Congress	http://www.loc.gov
Library of Congress: American Memory	https://memory.loc.gov/ammem/index.html
Library of Congress: Oral History Interviews	http://www.loc.gov/folklife/familyfolklife/oralhistory.html
Library of Congress: Teaching with Primary Sources	http://www.loc.gov/teachers/
Library Spot	http://www.libraryspot.com/

Lit2Go	http://etc.usf.edu/lit2go/
Metropolitan Museum of Art	http://www.metmuseum.org
National Archives and Records Administration	http://www.archives.gov/
National Archives: Document Analysis Worksheets	https://www.archives.gov/education/lessons/worksheets
National Geographic's Underground Railroad: Journey to Freedom	http://www.nationalgeographic.org/media/underground-railroad-journey-freedom/
National Museum of American History	http://americanhistory.si.edu/
National Park Service: Teaching with Historic Places	http://www.nps.gov/subjects/teachingwithhistoricplaces/index.htm
National World War II Museum: New Orleans	http://www.nationalww2museum.org
Oral History Association	http://www.oralhistory.org
Our Documents: 100 Milestone Documents	http://www.ourdocuments.gov
PBS	http://www.pbs.org
PBS Africans in America	http://www.pbs.org/wgbh/aia/home.html
PBS Kids Mad Money	http://pbskids.org/itsmylife/games/mad_money_flash.html
PBS Learning Media	http://www.pbslearningmedia.org/
PBS Online Learning	http://www.pbs.org/wnet/colonialhouse/history/
PBS's Slave Memories	http://www.pbs.org/wnet/slavery/memories/index_flash.html
Project Citizen	http://www.civiced.org/programs/project-citizen
Resources for Teaching American History	http://www.smithsoniansource.org
Scholastic's "Dear America"	http://www.scholastic.com/dearamerica/
Smithsonian Education	http://www.smithsonianeducation.org/
Smithsonian Source Resources for Teaching American History	http://www.smithsoniansource.org/
Tenement Museum New York City	http://www.tenement.org/tours.php
VocabularySpellingCity®	http://www.spellingcity.com/
Voki	http://www.voki.com/

Appendix D

Digital Resources

Blank templates of many of the charts in this book are available as Adobe PDF files. To access the digital resources, go to **www.tcmpub .com/download-files** and enter the code 97260702. Then, follow the on-screen directions.

Figure	Template Title	File Name
Figure 2.3	KWL Chart	KWL.pdf
Figure 2.5	Rate Your Knowledge Word Chart	rateknowledge.pdf
Figure 2.6	Predicting ABCs Chart	predictingABCs.pdf
Figure 3.1	Previewing the Textbook	previewingtextbook.pdf
Figure 3.4	It Says ... I Say ... And so ...	itsays.pdf
Figure 3.6	Somebody ... Wanted ... But ... So ...	somebodywantedbutso.pdf
Figure 3.7	Vocabulary Word Map 1	vocabwordmap1.pdf
Figure 3.8	Vocabulary Word Map 2	vocabwordmap2.pdf
Figure 3.9	Primary Frayer Model	primaryfrayer.pdf
Figure 3.10	Frayer Model	frayer.pdf

Figure	Template Title	File Name
Figure 3.11	Word Questioning	wordquestioning.pdf
Figure 3.12	H-diagram for Comparisons	Hdiagram.pdf
Figure 3.13	Concept Circle	conceptcircle.pdf
Figure 4.1	Advanced Organizer: T-Chart	advancedtchart.pdf
N/A	Narrative Planning Sheets	narrativeplanning.pdf
N/A	Claim ... Reason ... Evidence Graphic Organizer	claimreasonevidence.pdf
Figure 4.2	Advanced Organizer: Matrix	advancedmatrix.pdf
Figure 5.2	Comparing Now and Long Ago	comparingnowandlongago.pdf
Figure 5.3	Picture Study	picturestudy.pdf
Figure 6.7	Note-Taking Template	notetemplate.pdf
Figure 7.1	Chart to Record Observations and Inferences	recordobservationsandinferences.pdf
Figure 7.3	Historical Data Analysis Guide	historicaldataanalysis.pdf
Figure 8.2	Comparing Perspectives	comparingperspectives.pdf
Figure 9.5	Historical Advertisement Rubric	historicaladrubric.pdf
Figure 9.6	Rubric for Information Processing	infoprocessingrubric.pdf
Figure 9.7	Generic Information Rubric	genericinforubric.pdf
Figure 10.4	Data Retrieval Chart	dataretrievalchart.pdf

Notes

Notes